The Monster Called Grief

Sis Carol Nevins,

May God grant you

abundant blessings.

Love,

Anita Joy Sargeant

Please sign & date before
returning books to me. I
will be praying for you

THE MONSTER CALLED Grief

How to Deal with Grief and Support Others during Loss

ANITA JOY SARGEANT

IM PUBLISHING ™

The Monster Called Grief
How to Deal with Grief and Support Others during Loss
ISBN 978-0-615-86799-1
Copyright © 2014 by Anita Joy Sargeant

Published by Inspire Media
www.inspiremediallc.com

Cover Design:
Angela Carrington

All Scripture quotations are taken from the
King James Version of the Holy Bible.

All real life stories are fictional, based on true stories
of real people.

For more materials and products by Anita Joy Sargeant
please visit www.apostolicwinds.com.

*"I am not concerned that you have fallen;
I am concerned that you arise."*

— *Abraham Lincoln*

Contents

Acknowledgements

Thank you, Mom and Dad, for loving me and teaching me godly principles. That teaching has saved me much hurt.

Thanks to my niece, Michelle Ofori-Ansah, for reviewing this manuscript, giving some helpful advice, and writing a foreword. Her expertise in the area of counseling was particularly valuable as we searched for a proper critic. Michelle, you are so intelligent and so precious.

Thanks to my friend, Lorraine Brown Stoops, for all of the memories of time spent together laughing, crying, praying and sharing both the good times and the bad. Through it all, we are certain that Jesus cares and He makes a way.

Thank you, Becky Campora, for being there so many times when I hurt. You always know even from miles away just by the tone of my voice. I love you!

Thank you, Julie Carter, for giving me lots of feedback on this manuscript and for providing financial help to get it printed. You are a wonderful friend.

Thank you, dear Jesus, for being my Comforter and for never leaving, forsaking, rejecting, or betraying me. I love You most of all!

Dedication

I lovingly dedicate this volume to my family — brothers, sisters, nieces, and nephews. You mean so much to me. I enjoy getting together and talking about our childhood and our wonderful parents. They gave each of us such a rich heritage. My dream is to take their hands and with my life extend their influence to the next generation.

Nancy Hanks Lincoln and Her Son

"All that I am or ever shall hope to be,
I owe to my loving angel mother. God Bless her."

Abraham Lincoln

Michelle Ofori-Ansah

(Anita Joy Sargeant's niece)

Foreword

Like a monster, grief gnaws at the soul, crippling many and preventing them from pursuing a life of fulfillment and happiness. Their inability to deal with the loss of someone or something precious leaves them emotionally handicapped and ineffectual at home, at work, and in their daily pursuits. When I first heard the title The Monster Called Grief, I thought, "What a great title." However, The Monster Called Grief is not just an apt title for this book; it personifies the struggle many have in coping with grief and dealing with loss.

In this book, Anita Joy Sargeant gives you the tools to confront and break free from the grip of grief. As a Licensed Professional Counselor Intern, I have read any number of textbooks and journal articles about grief, the grief process, and how to approach that process as a helping professional. However, none of those have had the resonance, the personality, and the genuineness of this one. Most important, this book provides solutions for the everyday person. It is hard to put down and infinitely readable. Although it is written from a layperson's perspective, it brings truths from the counseling world into our ordinary lives.

Anita Sargeant has taken her extensive reading and mixed it with her natural helping ability as well as her own grieving process, and created something truly remarkable. Anita has written an accessible, humorous, and helpful book about grief; a book about grief that isn't sad or depressing. She combines sharing stories and provides real life examples with tested helping techniques for both the person dealing with grief and the person trying to help the grieving one.

This is the kind of book that once you read it, you want to recommend it to everyone you know . . . because everyone you know has dealt with grief, is dealing with grief, or is dealing with a friend or family member who is grieving. My only regret about this book is that it has not been published before now. The world desperately needs its approach to dealing with grief and grieving loved ones. I am glad that I have been able to be part of its inception. I hope it will be as impactful for you as it has been for me.

—**Michelle Ofori-Ansah**, MA, LPC-1

God Unfolds the Rose

It is only a tiny rosebud,
A flower of God's design;
But I cannot unfold the petals
With these clumsy hands of mine.

The secret of unfolding flowers
Is not known to such as I.
God opens this flower so easily,
But in my hands they die.

If I cannot unfold a rosebud,
This flower of God's design,
Then how can I have the wisdom
To unfold this life of mine?

So I'll trust in God for leading
Each moment of my day.
I will look to God for guidance
In each step along the way.

The path that lies before me,
Only my Lord and Savior knows.
I'll trust God to unfold the moments,
Just as He unfolds the rose.

—Unknown

Foreword

Anita Sargeant has written a masterpiece and a tool that can transform any life that has been touched by grief, if the concepts in this book are applied. She has used her personal experience, research, and counseling of the hurting to compose this timeless treasure.

I was privileged to know Anita during a very tragic time in my life. With her godly wisdom, prayers, and faithfulness to me as a friend, she was able to guide me through the grief process. If you will use this book as a guide, you too can make it to the other side of your grief no matter how great or small the circumstances that brought this monster into your life. You can defeat this monster and become even greater than before!

Thank you, Anita, for your burden and compassion for the hurting. You have birthed an instrument that will bring healing to many generations!

—Lorraine Y. Brown Stoops

Anita Joy Sargeant

Key Scripture

"The Spirit of the Lord is upon me, because he hath anointed me to preach the gospel to the poor; he hath sent me to heal the brokenhearted, to preach deliverance to the captives, and recovering of sight to the blind, to set at liberty them that are bruised" (Luke 4:18).

Preface

Grief visits all of us from time to time as we pass through life. Our response to grief is vital as it can make us either better or bitter. To become better we must offer our hurt on an altar of forgiveness and praise. It takes patience to do the will of God when we hurt. Time heals. Allowing time to do its work takes patience. This book helps us to understand and negotiate the time spent between pain and healing.

> *"Cast not away therefore your confidence, which hath great recompence of reward. For ye have need of patience, that, after ye have done the will of God, ye might receive the promise" (Hebrews 10:35-36).*

If we allow ourselves to become bitter we lose so much—relationships, peace, a clean conscience, and a joyful life.

A middle aged aunt often remarked to her nieces and nephews that all she wanted in life was to be a sweet old lady. It was difficult for the children to understand such a goal. As the aunt grew old, she contracted Alzheimer's disease. Though the disease was cruel and the years long, the family and the staff at the home where she lived marveled that she maintained such remarkable sweetness. Even in her weakened state the Holy Ghost responded to her desire to be a sweet old lady. When we consider the alternatives to being a sweet old lady, we understand the aunt's fervent desire was quite noble.

Our choices during times when we are strong and able determine our destiny once we lose control of our choices. Let's choose to respond to the monster called Grief in a manner that will make us better, not bitter. This race to gain the eternal prize will not be given to the one who runs the swiftest, nor to the one who shines for a day, but to the one who endures to the end.

For many years I have experienced the powerful hand of God working in my life. I have faced many difficult situations. Each time God has met me and helped me overcome them in a miraculous manner. I am deeply grateful. It is because of this that I write this book. I know that if God delivered me, He will deliver you as well. Many of the stories of real life trauma included in this book are my own. Others are those of dear friends. All of them are stories of real happenings. I have chosen to use pseudonyms and changed a few details to keep the personal references from distracting the reader from applying the examples to their own lives and to keep the identities of some of the characters private. If our suffering helps you in any way, the pain has been worth it.

> "For as the sufferings of Christ abound in us, so our consolation also aboundeth by Christ. And whether we be afflicted, it is for your consolation and salvation, which is effectual in the enduring of the same sufferings which we also suffer: or whether we be comforted, it is for your consolation and salvation. And our hope of you is stedfast, knowing, that as ye are partakers of the sufferings, so shall ye be also of the consolation" (II Corinthians 1:5-7).

Rock of Ages

Verse One
Rock of Ages, cleft for me,
Let me hide myself in Thee;
Let the water and the blood,
From Thy wounded side which flowed,
Be of sin the double cure,
Save from wrath and make me pure.

Verse Two
Could my tears forever flow,
Could my zeal no languor know,
These for sin could not atone;
Thou must save, and Thou alone:
In my hand no price I bring,
Simply to Thy cross I cling.

Verse Three
While I draw this fleeting breath,
When my eyes shall close in death,
When I rise to worlds unknown,
And behold Thee on Thy throne,
Rock of Ages, cleft for me,
Let me hide myself in Thee.

—*Augustus Toplady*

Understanding Grief

- The Anatomy of the Monster
- We Can't Fix Normal
- Grief and Family
- Grief and Temperament Differences
- A Gift of Hope

Chapter One

The Anatomy of the Monster

Jesus Heals the Brokenhearted

The monster called Grief visits each of us in varying ways throughout our lifetimes. He wears different clothes, comes to us when we least expect it, sneaks up and grabs us, and possibly screams, rants, and raves depending on his mood. Sometimes he slithers slowly into our lives like a snake and other times he comes to the front door, breaks it down, and roars like a lion as he enters. The most predictable thing about the monster called Grief is that he is unpredictable.

Whether we are grieving the loss of a well-manicured fingernail or the death of a child, we often run through the same stages of grief. The intensity of the loss determines how long it takes us to make it through the stages and how much we suffer. The passing of time is the key. Healing takes time.

If we are dealing with a small loss, the time we need to recover is relatively short and free of pain. If our loss is great, the time we need to recover takes longer and the pain may be torturous. The way we negotiate the feelings we face during the time Grief visits us determines our quality of life once the loss has been accepted and Grief is gone.

While negotiating grief and loss it is difficult to believe anyone understands what we face. Often well-meaning phrases of reassurance bring feelings of resentment as we silently ask, *"How would you know?"*

Suffering Turns into Compassion

While negotiating grief we may feel alone and forgotten. God may teach us to depend upon Him during the time we struggle to survive. If we respond correctly, our suffering turns into genuine compassion. Every drop of sorrow becomes gold to be used to further the cause of Christ.

I Walked a Mile with Sorrow

The following poem gives us insight as to why we may feel so alone during bouts with Grief.

I walked a mile with Pleasure,

She chattered all the way;

But left me none the wiser,

For all she had to say.

I walked a mile with Sorrow

And ne'er a word said she;

But, oh, the things I learned from her

When Sorrow walked with me!

—*Robert Browning Hamilton*

Stages of Grief

Though grief is a normal reaction to loss, and research predicts reactions to loss, recovery time varies. The stages are worked out personally with each circumstance and person. For the sake of study, we will separate grief into five stages. We introduce them in this chapter and deal with them more fully in later chapters.

Five Stages in the Grief Cycle:

➤ *Avoiding the Issue*

- *Lessens the immediate shock*
- *Comforts during the initial pain and aids survival*

➤ *Anger and Fear*

- *Emerges because the person feels helpless and unable to deal with the loss*
- *Often a grieving person misplaces anger and fear and may find targets in strangers or inanimate objects or even the friends and family who are trying to bring comfort*
- *Anger incites retaliation; fear causes the target to feel mistrusted*

➤ *Negotiating for a Change*

- *Seeks to regain control by negotiating*
- *May feel guilt or regret and express it by saying the words, "What if . . ."*

> ### *Depression and Discouragement*

- *Realizes loss cannot be reversed*
- *Enters a deep state of mourning*
- *Future looks bleak*
- *May feel suicidal*
- *Can be a beneficial time of deep soul searching and helps facilitate healing as it is incentive for change and keeps the individual from "going back to normal" or comfortable surroundings*

> ### *Acceptance and Redefining Reality*

- *Realizes the loss has brought about a permanent change*
- *Begins to let go of the past*
- *Forms new goals and relationships*

Looking the Monster in the Face

No matter what causes grief the accompanying feelings are very real. A simple command to "Get over it!" does nothing to relieve the pain. Only enduring the process and responding to the various stages brings us to a place of acceptance. The time we spend moving from one stage to another varies.

We may go back and forth from one stage to another randomly. It is especially common to revisit a previous stage, albeit for a short period of time, even after we have "finished" that stage. (There is more information on this subject in chapter six.)

Recovery from loss widely varies as the monster called Grief visits for various reasons. Let's explore reasons and recall times in our lives when we have faced Grief. Though this list is long, there are many other causes for grief. We may or may not find our cause of grief on this list.

> *Moving to a new location*
>   - *Loss of family or friends*
>   - *Loss of familiar household belongings*
>   - *Loss of familiar geographic areas*

> *Disappointment due to unrealized goals or dreams*
>   - *Self-imposed goals or dreams*
>   - *Job-related goals or dreams*
>   - *Family-related goals or dreams*
>   - *Church-related goals or dreams*

> *Rejection or betrayal from those we care about*
>   - *Change of lifestyle or dreams due to imposed distance*
>   - *Pain caused by misunderstanding, lies, or inflicted pain*
>   - *Distance imposed due to fear and lack of trust*
>   - *Hesitance to rebuild due to fear of being hurt again*

➢ **Prejudice**

- Preconceived notions that exclude generally because of race, color, or gender

➢ **Catastrophic Event**

- Due to vehicle or other accident
- Due to weather-related event
- Due to fire, storm, or other destructive force

➢ **Loss of job or income**

- Imposed lifestyle change
- Loss of familiar schedule
- Loss of familiar work environment
- Loss of work associates

➢ **Loss of health or strength**

- Loss of job and income
- Change of schedule and familiar surroundings
- Pain in body with accompanying stress
- Facing a doctor's negative prognosis

➢ **Loss of family or loved one due to death**

- Guilt and shame, self-imposed or imposed by another
- Regret due to unfulfilled desires
- Change of lifestyle
- Loneliness

Keeping the Monster from Moving In

Though the monster called Grief is real and he may visit often in life, it is important to put Grief in his place. To invite him into our lives to live is a big mistake. He may roar, rant, and rave leaving a destructive path. He may shake us at our very foundation but he is an unwelcome visitor and does not have the right to take up residence. Keeping this in mind gives us a glimmer of hope even in the darkest night.

Points to Ponder

> ➤ *The monster called Grief visits each of us in varying ways during our lifetime.*

> ➤ *The intensity of the loss determines how long it takes us to make it through the stages of grief and how much we suffer.*

> ➤ *Healing takes time.*

> ➤ *While negotiating grief and loss, it is difficult to believe others understand what we face.*

> ➤ *If we respond correctly, suffering turns into compassion.*

> ➤ *Though we all react to grief differently, there are some predictable stages of grief.*

> ➤ *There are many causes for grief.*

> ➤ *It is important that we do not let Grief move into our lives permanently.*

Prayers

> ➢ *Jesus, it is difficult for me to face the monster called Grief with faith. Would you help me believe You will sustain me through this terrible loss?*

> ➢ *Lord, I don't know how long it will take me to make it through this. It is difficult to have patience. Would you help me not to lose heart?*

> ➢ *I know healing takes time. I am trying to accept that fact.*

> ➢ *God, it feels as though no one understands what I am going through. I feel all alone.*

> ➢ *Lord, I know suffering turns into compassion if I respond correctly. I want to do Your perfect will.*

> ➢ *Though I know that for decades others have suffered, that knowledge does little to help me now. My grief is so fresh and so real.*

> ➢ *Jesus, I believe someday I will come to a place of acceptance and this monster called Grief will be gone. Would You help me maintain my integrity with You until that day comes?*

Molly's Trust Is Betrayed

Story of Real Life Trauma

Molly's parents discussed a disturbing problem as they made their way outside from the church basement and down the sidewalk, planning to reenter the Sunday service in progress in the upper-level auditorium.

"I want up, Daddy, please?" two-year-old Molly begged as her daddy scooped her up. Molly's mama, very close to delivering their fourth child, walked closest to the street as they made their way down the sidewalk toward the church entrance.

The father, who suffered from an unexplained but serious medical condition and possibly over-reacting to the stress of the discussion, hastily thrust two-year-old Molly toward her mother; in her condition, the mother could not catch the baby hurled at her so unexpectedly. Molly's head struck a parked car, resulting in a minor head wound. Fear gripped the two-year-old as her head began to bleed profusely, causing anxiety and confusion in her young heart.

Molly stood on the sidewalk analyzing the situation from her point of view. "Why did I ask Daddy to pick me up? I can walk. This is my fault. I have learned a lesson. I will never let another man pick me up again," she vowed, and endeavored from that day forth to keep the vow.

Nowhere Else to Go by Nathan Greene

"I have been driven many times upon my knees by the overwhelming conviction that I had nowhere else to go. My own wisdom and that of all about me seemed insufficient for that day."

— *Abraham Lincoln*

Chapter Two

We Can't Fix Normal

Jesus Heals the Brokenhearted

Whether the monster called Grief visits us over death of a loved one, severe illness, separation from those we love, betrayal, financial hardship, or other of life's dilemmas, the process for recovery is similar. A difficult hurdle is the realization that there is no quick fix.

What Does Normal Mean?

If we are the one suffering, it may feel as if we will never recover. "Normal" is just a word we know about, not a feeling we experience. We wonder if we are going crazy as thoughts swirl through our heads like legions of demons.

Our natural reaction when we become aware of the pain of a loved one is to fix it so it doesn't hurt anymore. Someone once said, *"We can't fix normal."* It is normal to hurt during times of loss. Offering our support should be our goal rather than fixing it so we can get on with other activities.

Reaching for Fragments of Hope

When we reach for fragments of hope or try to offer hope to someone who is grieving, we may accidentally suppress or assist others in suppressing the natural, normal process that must be faced to gain acceptance of the loss. This process takes time. Giving ourselves or others permission to hurt or to grieve is a precious gift.

What Is Wrong with Me?

We may feel we are "wrong" or "bad" for grieving, or we may accidentally cause others to feel they are "wrong" or "bad" for feeling the normal hurt of a grieving heart.

It's Okay to Hurt

One way we may assist is to say words like, "It's okay to hurt" or "It's okay to cry" or "It's okay to make some reasonable allowances for yourself during this difficult time." We can't fix normal no matter how we try.

When we hurt it often helps to express it in some manner. Telling someone else that we know will listen and understand may ease the pain.

Points to Ponder

➤ *There is no quick fix for the problem when Grief comes to call.*

➤ *Grief causes us to lose sight of "normal."*

➤ *Giving ourselves or others permission to hurt or grieve is a precious gift.*

➤ *A visit from Grief does not happen because we are "wrong" or "bad." It is just part of life.*

➤ *It is okay to hurt.*

➤ *When we hurt it often helps to express it in some manner.*

Prayers

➤ *Jesus, I feel so confused and want all this pain to go away. I want it to be over.*

➤ *I don't even know what normal is anymore.*

➤ *I want to know You do not blame me for this visit from Grief.*

➤ *I hope I haven't done anything wrong. If so, would You forgive me? If not, would You deal with this accused feeling I am struggling with? I want to feel clean in Your sight.*

➤ *Jesus, I am reaching to You for comfort today. I am hurting.*

"You cannot escape the responsibility
of tomorrow by evading it today."

— Abraham Lincoln

Sally's Father Dies

Story of Real Life Trauma

At five years old, Sally looked around for some way to see into her father's casket. She and her sisters stood quietly by and watched the strangers and loved ones as they peered into what the grown-ups called the "casket." Sally longed for someone to help her—to pick her up and allow her to see what they saw when they looked inside. She had been told her daddy was in there and that he was dead.

Finally, when the people had passed and it seemed no one was looking, Sally hoisted herself up on the side of the casket to look at her daddy for the last time. She longed to feel close to him. She did not know his corpse would be cold. Her face was very close to the body and her perch was precarious but she gingerly reached out and touched his fingers. Sally instantly yanked her hand away in horror as the cold body forced her to understand the finality of death.

Sally nearly fell off of the railing under the casket where she had perched. She caught herself with her hands as they gripped the side of the casket, then she quietly slipped to the floor and rejoined her sisters standing solemnly in a line nearby. She felt betrayed and abandoned. She didn't know how to decipher her feelings. This was her first head-on encounter with the monster called Grief.

Chapter Three

Grief and Family

Jesus Heals the Brokenhearted

Will We Draw Close or Splinter Away?

During crisis families survive and become closer or they splinter away from one another. Either they comfort one another to compensate for the loss or they accuse and blame and become distant. It seems the monster called Grief would like to break up homes and friendships. We can bind together to fight against him when he tries his tricks. We can make intelligent and godly choices when faced with decisions that will either alienate us from family and friends or bring us closer to them.

We Grieve in Different Ways

Because we are made so differently with various inherited tendencies, we grieve differently even if we are in the same family grieving over the same loss. Offering others permission to react and feel differently than we do as we deal with our tragedies helps bring understanding and healing.

I Am Just Trying to Help

Family commitment makes it natural to reach out and try to ease the pain and sorrow of loved ones. When others try to help they may do the wrong thing. If we consciously respond to the nurturing feeling and refuse to be offended as family members do their best, it inspires healing and recovery instead of pain and destruction. It is healthy to understand we (and others) may make mistakes even when we (and they) are just trying to help.

Doing the Right Thing Is Difficult

Interacting with one another during crisis is difficult. When we feel pain we may withdraw to hide away and nurse our wounds. We may long to be with family or friends but feel we do not have the tools to give to the relationship so we turn down invitations and make remarks like "I'm OK," or we may even snap, "Why do you keep checking on me?"

Whether we are dealing with the natural family or the spiritual family, meeting needs during crises is difficult. Deep sorrow and loss carry with them confusion, pain of emotional frustration, financial hardship, and physical trauma. We may find the task monumental as we struggle to conquer our own challenges and bear the burdens of our brothers and sisters as well. Even so, the effort is worth it.

"Bear ye one another's burdens, and so fulfil the law of Christ" (Galatians 6:2).

Points to Ponder

- ➢ *During crises families survive and become closer or they splinter away from one another.*

- ➢ *We all grieve differently.*

- ➢ *Sometimes when we try to help, we offend.*

- ➢ *Sometimes when someone tries to help us they hurt us.*

- ➢ *It is a struggle to do the right thing when Grief comes to visit.*

Prayers

- ➢ *Jesus, our family has faced a terrible tragedy. We are all so hurt and confused. Would You help us to become closer as we heal? We don't want to face another tragedy on top of this one.*

- ➢ *Lord, I don't understand some of my family members. They don't seem to know what helps me to feel better and I can't seem to figure out how to tell them. Would You help us to be patient and understanding with one another?*

- ➢ *I am sorry I hurt my family members when I was trying to help. Please forgive me.*

- ➢ *Would You give me a forgiving heart when friends and family treat me in a manner that adds pain to my already grieving soul?*

"Always bear in mind that your own resolution to succeed is more important than any other."
— *Abraham Lincoln*

Chad's Grandmother Dies
Story of Real Life Trauma

Eleven-year-old Chad listened in horror to his mother's phone conversation: "Is she really that sick, sis.?" then a long pause … "They don't expect her to live through the night.? We will come right away then." Chad knew Mom was talking to his Aunt Jane about his grandmother.

Grandmother was a great lady. Always so industrious! When she came to visit she baked the best goodies, just like he and his brothers liked. She also knitted, tatted, crocheted, and sewed. She could take a little bit of nothing and come up with a sweater, stockings, mittens, doilies, and even little stuffed animals. Chad mused about the time she made each of the grandchildren a little stuffed animal out of an old, white yarn coat. She worked hard to make them just right. When Chad opened his gift that Christmas he tried to be happy and keep it from her that he felt disappointed.

Mom hung up the phone and looked at Chad sadly. "Chad, we have bad news. They do not expect your grandmother to live through the night." Chad stared at his mother and his throat constricted. He ran for the stairs and retreated into his room.

"Jesus," he prayed as he lay across the bed sobbing. "I don't want Grandmother to die!" In a few moments Chad felt the comforting Spirit of God wash over him giving him strength and help for the crisis.

Chapter Four

Grief and Temperament Differences

Jesus Heals the Brokenhearted

God made us all unique—different from one another. When the monster called Grief comes to visit, we all react differently. Understanding those differences may be helpful as we struggle to deal with our own grief at the same time as we work to maintain meaningful relationships.

The more we respect differences of those we love and learn to react intelligently, the better we will deal with the monster called Grief. When we respect differences we do more for others and we have less conflict in our lives. God made us all different; however, for the sake of study we will observe four basic temperaments, or inherited tendencies. None of these should be considered "good" or "bad" temperaments, just different.

Personality vs. Temperament

Understanding our basic inherited tendencies may help develop our personality. Personality is formed by what we do with inherited temperament. Two people with the same basic inherited temperaments may have different personalities because of differences in background, circumstance, and their level of submission to God and His Word.

We are stuck with inherited temperament, but not with a particular personality. Through the Spirit we can overcome our weaknesses and strengthen our strengths. Most people have a drastic change in personality when they receive the Holy Ghost and begin to walk in the Spirit! Changes continue as they submit to the principles of God's Word.

For example, some may have inherited a temperament that makes it difficult to forgive, but when they realize God expects us to forgive one another, they can, through the Spirit, forgive on a consistent basis.

The truth according to God's Word reveals none of us are any good without the Holy Ghost. No study of self-esteem or positive thinking changes that fact. If we do not walk in the Spirit, we will yield to the lust of the flesh.

> *"For all flesh is as grass, and all the glory of man as the flower of grass. The grass withereth, and the flower thereof falleth away: but the word of the Lord endureth for ever. And this is the word which by the gospel is preached unto you"* *(I Peter 1:24-25)*.

Jesus gives a beautiful reminder and a promise. We are nothing without Him, but we bear much fruit if we abide in Him.

> *"I am the vine, ye are the branches: He that abideth in me, and I in him, the same bringeth forth much fruit: for without me ye can do nothing"* *(John 15:5)*.

Introduction to Temperament Types

Dr. Tim LaHaye caused the ancient concept of four major temperament types to be popular in the United States during the past century. His books *Why You Act the Way You Do* and *Spirit Controlled Temperaments* helped many understand themselves. We may have characteristics from each temperament type, but most of us are a combination of two types, one being more predominant than the other.

These *four temperament types* include two that are more *socially oriented* and two that are more *work oriented. Two are extroverts* and *two are introverts.* There are many differences but these are the main divisions. For instance, everyone is social and everyone needs to work, but some temperaments do one or the other more naturally, making the human race work together as a productive functioning body. If we all lead, who would follow? If we all followed, who would lead?

Traditionally, the two more *social temperaments* have been referred to as *Sanguine* and *Phlegmatic*, the Sanguine being an extrovert and therefore an initiator and the Phlegmatic being an introvert and therefore a responder.

The other two are more *work oriented*, the *Choleric* being an extrovert and more production minded and the *Melancholy* being an introvert and more research minded.

The *introverted* temperaments are more apt to be *fearful* and the *extroverted* temperaments are more apt to be *angry*, often for the same reasons. When the monster called Grief visits the introverted temperaments, they tend to cower in fear. When he visits the extroverted temperaments they are more apt to lash out with anger. Both are caused by the helpless feelings brought about by the visit from Grief.

We Need Each Other

Each temperament needs the other temperaments to complement their own. We have all attended events with a friend and experienced the same things, yet when we come back we each tell the story differently. Why is this? Are some of us right and others wrong? Not necessarily! Some may merely have a different perspective than others.

We are not always right when we make suppositions about others based on our own thoughts and feelings. This can cause misunderstandings and hurt feelings that may take years to dispel.

> *"A brother offended is harder to be won than a strong city: and their contentions are like the bars of a castle" (Proverbs 18:19).*

Our natural strengths are not necessarily the strengths of those closest to us; likewise, our natural weaknesses are not necessarily the same as the people around us. Our strengths are not better than someone else's or inferior to another's, but different. We must guard against excusing our weaknesses because it is hard to overcome them by saying, "That's just the way I am!" This is especially dangerous if our weaknesses lead us to sin.

If we through the Spirit overcome those parts of our nature that do not line up with the Word of God, we can truly be children of God.

"For if ye live after the flesh, ye shall die: but if ye through the Spirit do mortify the deeds of the body, ye shall live. For as many as are led by the Spirit of God, they are the sons of God" (Romans 8:13-14).

All Things to All Men

Although the concept of four different temperaments and various thinking patterns are not specifically recorded in the Bible, Jesus, as well as the apostle Paul, gave us an example of being all things to all men that we might win souls.

"To the weak became I as weak, that I might gain the weak: I am made all things to all men, that I might by all means save some. And this I do for the gospel's sake, that I might be partaker thereof with you" (I Corinthians 9:22-23).

Jesus did not always react to people in the same manner; even in similar circumstances. It is interesting to note when Lazarus died Martha and Mary both came to Jesus and said exactly the same words.

"Lord, if thou hadst been here, my brother had not died" (John 11:21, 32).

Jesus' response to each of them was notably different. He reasoned with Martha and did His best to explain what was going on. When Mary spoke the same words, Jesus wept. He made no attempt to reason with her but let her know with His tears that He cared.

We all need other people. Some temperaments need people more than others do. Some need people more than they think they do, and for different reasons than other temperaments do.

An awareness of specific differences adds tolerance and helps us adapt to others. However, we must guard against specifically categorizing others or ourselves and realize God made many different types of people. Although we may separate types for the sake of study, most people are a combination unlike anyone anywhere.

Comparison Is Not Wise

Although all temperaments have many beautiful strengths, they all have serious weaknesses that can be overcome only by walking in the Spirit. We should never accept sin in our lives or condone it in others, but we do need to accept differences. Comparing ourselves with someone else is not wise. We will either feel excited with pride because of the comparison or feel like a failure.

God made us all different for special purposes. A study of our own temperament helps us overcome those areas where we need particular help from God and from fellow saints. It also gives us confidence to do those things we have the ability to do well. A careful look at human nature can make us much more effective in soulwinning and in our relationships with family and friends.

Adjusting our reaction to the person or the circumstance at hand is essential to being the friend that supports rather than the one that adds stress to the already impossible situation.

> *"Rejoice with them that do rejoice, and weep with them that weep"* (Romans 12:15).

Learning to weep with those who weep may be difficult. Though the Melancholy may find it easier than the Sanguine or the Choleric, it takes selflessness from anyone to pause and take time to comfort those who are hurting. The impetus for success is experience. Pain turns into compassion if we react in a positive manner.

Choleric Temperament and Grief

The outspoken, choleric, take-charge, production-minded temperament is generally the most apt to dismiss the monster called Grief as simply a bother and pay little  attention to him. He is not easily ruffled and Grief is just another imposter to be trifled with. This works for him most of the time but catches up with him on the heavy stuff. His sympathy for others often doesn't go too deep unless he has been hurt badly by some great loss in his life. He may be heard saying, "Just get over it!" or something similar.

Sanguine Temperament and Grief

The outgoing, sanguine, talker, social, idealist, temperament is often crushed momentarily when visited by Grief but soon they find a distraction that keeps them from succumbing long to the power of the monster. Circumstances may plunge them into a place where the monster reenters because they don't lock the door when they kick him out. Soon they realize an intruder is there and will kick him out again and possibly again and again.

Their reaction when dealing with friends in their grief may be to find them good activities to distract them. If the person is outgoing, this may be a welcome antidote. If the person is more introverted, they may decline the invitation, feel offended, or think the person doesn't care. The Sanguine often accepts the griever's decline with a shrug and moves on to another more interesting activity.

Melancholy Temperament and Grief

The introverted, melancholy, detailed, research-minded, deep thinker, temperament often cowers in fear when faced by the monster called Grief. They are further traumatized when one of the more outgoing temperaments looks down on him for his cowering tendencies. They look into the past and visit and revisit the reason the monster came. They blame themselves and possibly others. They mull it over and over and over, actually reveling in the process. If they are not careful Grief will move his belongings into their houses and stay there for the rest of their lives. It will take determination, will power, and courage to kick the monster out the door, lock it, and keep him from reentering.

No other temperament is so able to understand when someone feels a need for sympathy because of a visit from Grief. The Melancholy will listen long and will help to make as much sense as possible out of the disaster or tragedy. He may do such a good job he ends up hanging a shingle and making a living. Melancholies are the most apt to say the right thing at the right time to help a person in distress.

Phlegmatic Temperament and Grief

The introverted, soft-spoken, phlegmatic, sweet, peaceful, watcher, negotiator-minded temperament will shudder in fear as the monster called Grief approaches. If possible, they will retreat, avoid the issue, and stay there as long as possible. When they are forced to face the changes made by the monster, they will grieve quietly and may enjoy the company of the Melancholy as they are drawn out to face the tragedy.

Sometimes the Phlegmatic gets stuck in the first stage of grief and stays for a long period before moving on to the other stages and finally accepting the trauma to the point they can kick the monster called Grief out the door and lock it for good.

When others are faced with trauma, the Phlegmatic may help them retreat to a place of avoiding the issue instead of leading them on to a place of acceptance. Their fear of the monster and lack of self-confidence may keep them from actually becoming involved in helping their friends in time of grief. They are more apt to avoid the person. The reaction of the friend who is grieving is to feel abandoned and possibly hurt because they feel ignored, rejected, or forgotten.

Conclusion

The Choleric tells us, "Get over it!" The Sanguine wants to find something more interesting or fun to get involved with; the Melancholy wants to make a science out of it and possibly charge us an arm and a leg; and the Phlegmatic retreats into hiding. This knowledge is interesting and may add some tolerance to our reactions but does little to comfort us when Grief comes to call.

It takes supernatural power from God to overcome our natural tendencies and reach out to find help, or to help others in time of need. This is available through the gifts of the Spirit and the five-fold ministry.

It takes patience with our friends to keep from becoming angry and distant with them when they do not respond to us in a manner that helps us as we battle Grief. Often their reactions add stress instead of alleviating it.

Points to Ponder

➤ *God made us different from one another. We are all unique.*

➤ *When we understand and respect differences, it is easier to help ourselves and support one another during times of loss.*

➤ *Personality is formed by what we do with inherited temperament.*

➤ *Most people have a drastic change in personality when they receive the Holy Ghost and begin to walk in the Spirit!*

➤ *We all need each other.*

➤ *Most of us are a combination of two temperament types, one being more predominant than the other.*

➤ *The two more social temperaments have been referred to as Sanguine and Phlegmatic.*

➤ *The two more work-oriented temperaments have been referred to as Choleric and Melancholy.*

➤ *The introverted temperaments are more apt to be fearful, the extroverted to be angry and often for the same reasons.*

➤ *Comparing ourselves with someone else and feeling either excited with pride or like a failure is not wise.*

➤ *The Choleric tends to treat the monster called Grief as an imposter. Little ruffles him and Grief is a trifle to be dealt with unless the tragedy is huge.*

➤ *The Sanguine is crushed momentarily when visited by Grief but soon finds a distraction that keeps him from succumbing long to the power of the monster.*

➤ *The Melancholy may allow Grief to move his belongings into his house and stay there for the rest of his life. It takes determination, will power, and courage for him to kick the monster out the door, lock it, and keep him from reentering.*

➤ *The Melancholy temperament is better able to understand when someone feels a need for sympathy because of a visit from Grief. He may even make a living doing it.*

➤ *When we become involved with the supernatural power of God we are able to overcome tragedies and help others during loss.*

Prayers

➤ *Jesus, thank You for making me different from anyone else. I am Your special child.*

➤ *I want to understand and respect the fact that everyone I know does not think and feel the way I do. Would You teach me to respect and value that fact and respond accordingly?*

➤ *Lord, I have faults and I have strong points. Would you help me overcome my faults through the power of Your Spirit and to thank You for my strengths without becoming proud and arrogant?*

➤ *Thank You for the power of the Holy Ghost! Without You I can do nothing; through You I shall do valiantly.*

➤ *I find I am mostly these two temperaments:*

_____.

Would You help me to overcome the weaknesses and sharpen the strengths so my life is useful in Your kingdom? Right now my desire is to understand how this affects the trauma I am facing.

> *Father, I want to be mightily used by God by becoming involved in the supernatural power of God through the gifts of the Spirit and the five-fold ministry. Thank You for providing such powerful tools. I love You!*

Nowhere Else to Go by Nathan Greene

Nikki's Boyfriend Has a Tragic Accident
Story of Real Life Trauma

Twenty-five year-old Nikki had been dating a young man named John from a nearby city. Though they were not making serious plans for marriage at that point, they both enjoyed the budding friendship.

One evening as Nikki drove home from work, the Lord spoke to her: "Nikki, what would you do if someone you cared for was killed in a motorcycle accident?"

She replied, "It would be very difficult to accept."

"Will you allow me to be Lord of your life, no matter what you face?" Nikki began in that moment to weep and surrender to Him. When she arrived home, she received a call telling her that John had been killed in a motorcycle accident. His family, being Catholic, decided on a closed funeral. Even a proper goodbye was forbidden.

As Nikki grieved she looked to the heavens and whispered a prayer: "Jesus, thank You for warning me about this so I was not caught off guard. Thank You for being close to me and comforting me during loss. It is so difficult to be forbidden even a simple goodbye. It seems so unfair. Please help me to forgive. Amen."

Chapter Five

A Gift of Hope

Jesus Heals the Brokenhearted

W ithin every one of us is a desire to thrive — survival is an instinct. Part of that instinct is what one author called "A Gift of Hope."

In explaining how we survive tragedy, Robert Veninga states:

> *Philosophers have long suggested that there exists within each of us a reservoir of hope. Ralph Waldo Emerson once noted that in our core we are prepared to recreate the whole world out of ourselves even if no one else existed. What is it that creates this kind of optimism?*
>
> *In* The Revolution of Hope, *Erich Fromm presents a straightforward thesis: Hope is basic to man's existence. 'Does the infant not hope to stand erect and to walk? Does the sick man not hope to get well, the prisoner to be free, the hungry to eat? Do we not hope to wake up to another day when we fall asleep?'*
>
> *Within the essence of our being there is, to use a Hegelian concept, a real possibility that life can change for the better. The word possible as it is used here does not signify*

abstract possibility, nor does it mean projecting dreams that do not have a basis in fact.

Rather, a real possibility means that others facing equally troubling situations have been able to transcend their loss (A Gift of Hope, How We Survive Our Tragedies, *Robert L. Veninga 1985, p. 78*).

When tragedy strikes something deep down inside wants to believe we will be all right. It is connected with our will to live. Our will to live is connected to our desire to please God and keep His commandments. We all have a deep longing inspiring us to seek after God—to find Him to be a personal God involved in our everyday activities.

Life Is Full of Trouble

If we only have hope in life on earth we soon become discouraged because we find as years go by our bodies are not as strong and able as during our prime. Life is full of trouble and heartache to be overcome.

"Man that is born of a woman is of few days, and full of trouble" (Job 14:1).

Hope of Eternal
Life Brings Comfort

The Christian who maintains hope in life eternal feels the comfort of something wonderful to come in the future.

"If in this life only we have hope in Christ, we are of all men most miserable" (I Corinthians 15:19).

We understand life is a vapor appearing for a short time and then it is gone. We are challenged to give our will to God. He does not force us to serve Him but longs for us to draw near and find grace to help in time of need.

"Let us therefore come boldly unto the throne of grace, that we may obtain mercy, and find grace to help in time of need" (Hebrews 4:16).

In His Presence Is Fullness of Joy

Through the power of the Holy Ghost we have a small taste of what it will be like to live forever with Jesus in Heaven.

"In whom ye also trusted, after that ye heard the word of truth, the gospel of your salvation: in whom also after that ye believed, ye were sealed with that holy Spirit of promise, which is the earnest of our inheritance until the redemption of the purchased possession, unto the praise of his glory" (Ephesians 1:13-14).

We experience a taste of what is to come when we feel the refreshing presence of the Lord wash over us, providing comfort and a host of other benefits.

"Thou wilt shew me the path of life: in thy presence is fulness of joy; at thy right hand there are pleasures for evermore" (Psalm 16:11).

When we allow the joy of the Lord to fill our souls through the refreshing that comes with daily prayer, we have strength to face the future. The joy of the Lord is our strength.

> *"Then he said unto them, Go your way, eat the fat, and drink the sweet, and send portions unto them for whom nothing is prepared: for this day is holy unto our Lord: neither be ye sorry; for the joy of the LORD is your strength"* *(Nehemiah 8:10).*

Hope and Faith Are Intertwined

Hope is part faith—a very important part of an overcomer's life. Faith is the substance of things we hope for. Hope is a seed growing into something supernatural—faith.

> *"Now faith is the substance of things hoped for, the evidence of things not seen"* *(Hebrews 11:1).*

Without hope, we would never have faith. Without faith it is impossible to please God.

> *"But without faith it is impossible to please him: for he that cometh to God must believe that he is, and that he is a rewarder of them that diligently seek him"* *(Hebrews 11:6).*

"In the end, it's not the years in your life that count. It's the life in your years."

— *Anonymous*

Points to Ponder

➢ *When tragedy strikes, something deep down inside of us wants to believe we will be all right.*

➢ *Life is full of trouble and heartache that must be overcome.*

➢ *If we have hope only in this life, we are miserable.*

➢ *Hope of eternal life brings comfort.*

➢ *The Holy Ghost baptism is the earnest of our inheritance.*

➢ *In His presence is fullness of joy.*

➢ *Hope is a seed growing into something supernatural—faith.*

Prayers

➢ *Jesus, thank You for putting the gift of hope deep in our hearts to help us when tragedy strikes.*

➢ *Lord, this life is full of trouble. I have joy in my heart and hope for the future only because of You.*

➢ *I am so grateful for the benefits given to the Holy Ghost filled child of God. I feel Your comfort today. I feel the joy of the Lord crowding out the grief and giving me hope for the future.*

➢ *Your joy gives me strength. Oh how I love You!*

> *As hope that life will be better takes hold, I feel a supernatural touch of faith filling my soul. I know everything will be all right. Thank You, Jesus!*

"The rage I nurture is often one-sided, for my offender seldom gives thought to his offense."

— *Anonymous*

I Know Who Holds Tomorrow

Verse One

I don't know about tomorrow,
I just live from day to day;
I don't borrow from its sunshine,
For its skies may turn to gray.
I don't worry o'er the future,
For I know what Jesus said,
And today I'll walk beside Him,
For He knows what is ahead.

Verse Two

Ev'ry step is getting brighter
As the golden stairs I climb;
Ev'ry burden's getting lighter,
Ev'ry cloud is silver-lined.
There the sun is always shining,
There no tear will dim the eye,
At the ending of the rainbow,
Where the mountains touch the sky.

Verse Three

I don't know about tomorrow,
It may bring me poverty;
But the one who feeds the sparrow,
Is the one who stands by me.
And the path that is my portion,
May be through the flame or flood,
But His presence goes before me,
And I'm covered with the blood.

Chorus

Many things about tomorrow
I don't seem to understand;
But I know who holds tomorrow,
And I know who holds my hand.

—Ira F. Stanphill

"The best thing about the future is that it comes one day at a time."

— Abraham Lincoln

Negotiating Grief

- The Slippery Slopes of Grief
- Waves of Grief
- Avoiding the Issue
  —*Stage One*
- Anger and Fear
  —*Stage Two*
- Negotiating for a Change
  —*Stage Three*
- Depression and Discouragement
  —*Stage Four*
- Acceptance and Redefining
  Reality —*Stage Five*

Chapter Six

The Slippery Slopes of Griefe

Jesus Heals the Brokenhearted

As we review the five stages of grief we remember that dealing with grief is like going up and down slippery slopes. The pathway is sometimes difficult to establish. Just when  we feel one stage is conquered we may find ourselves at the top of the hill, beginning to slide down again.

Though we refer to five stages in the grief process, the person grieving may not necessarily begin with stage one and sequentially walk through each stage in a predictable manner. He or she may go through each stage more than once, skip stages, or walk through them randomly.

Revisiting Painful Memories

Different life circumstances stare us in the face, demanding that we revisit painful memories. This may throw us back into the grief cycle again. For example, in the case of a loved one who died, subsequent holidays or birthdays may trigger memories and inflict pain. Habits that always included another person who is no longer there may bring additional grief.

In the case of betrayal or separation, subsequent life circumstances may force those persons to be together again, triggering grief. For example, in the case of a divorced couple, birthdays, anniversaries, graduations, weddings, funerals, holidays, and other events inflict additional pain because of the memories they evoke.

Healing Happens in Layers

Healing often happens in layers. We can feel as though the monster called Grief has been kicked out for good, but suddenly life circumstances fling open the door and the monster comes charging into our lives with vengeance. We may feel discouraged and say, "I thought I was healed in this area." The truth is that healing did come but another layer of the pain that caused the hurt has resurfaced to be dealt with.

When speaking of healing Jesus referred to the bruised. The bruised are those who are brokenhearted. Bruises heal in layers. It takes time. They change color and look different in the various stages. The larger they are the more pain they inflict and the longer it takes to heal. A large bruise hurts more in the center than it does on the peripherals. These thoughts apply when we consider the healing of the brokenhearted.

> *"The Spirit of the Lord is upon me, because he hath anointed me to preach the gospel to the poor; he hath sent me to heal the brokenhearted, to preach deliverance to the captives, and recovering of sight to the blind, to set at liberty them that are bruised" (Luke 4:18).*

"Tact is the ability to describe others as they see themselves."

— *Abraham Lincoln*

Points to Ponder

➤ *Dealing with grief is often like going up and down slippery slopes. The path is not clear.*

➤ *Life circumstances plunge us into places where we often revisit painful memories.*

➤ *Healing for broken hearts happens in layers much as a bruise heals.*

Prayers

➤ *Jesus, my pathway seems so dark and slippery. I feel I cannot find my way.*

➤ *Just when I felt I was beginning to heal, Grief has overwhelmed me again. I am struggling to make it through this, Jesus. Would You help me?*

➤ *I believe You can and will heal me, Jesus. You promised to heal the brokenhearted. I love You!*

Tis So Sweet to Trust in Jesus

Verse One

'Tis so sweet to trust in Jesus,

Just to take Him at His Word;

Just to rest upon His promise;

Just to know, "Thus saith the Lord."

Chorus

Jesus, Jesus, how I trust Him!

How I've proved Him o'er and o'er!

Jesus, Jesus, precious Jesus!

O for grace to trust Him more!

Verse Two

O how sweet to trust in Jesus,

Just to trust His cleansing blood;

Just in simple faith to plunge me

'Neath the healing, cleansing flood!

Verse Four

I'm so glad I learned to trust Thee,

Precious, Jesus, Savior, Friend;

And I know that Thou art with me,

Wilt be with me to the end.

— **William Kirkpatrick**

Chapter Seven

Waves of Grief

Jesus Heals the Brokenhearted

Just as the waves of the sea come crashing in and then retreat only to build momentum and then come crashing back, even so when the monster  called Grief comes to visit he crashes through our lives repeatedly at the most unexpected moments.

Often we momentarily forget he is there and are actually caught off guard when he comes crashing back into our view, making grief our focus no matter how inconvenient it may be at the moment.

Trigger Points

Grief is often propelled into action by various trigger points. Sometimes it is a new event, familiar smell, sight, habit, piece of clothing, familiar place, mutual friend, recurring event, or holiday. We often are caught off guard as we do not foresee that the trigger point will activate grief until the monster has entered the room, taken control, and disrupted whatever we were in the process of doing.

This aspect of grief is often one of the most difficult to bear. If we could schedule his visits to occur when we had time and felt prepared possibly we would never schedule them, but if we did we would be prepared for the onslaught. The rude entrances of the monster at the most unexpected moments are almost unbearable.

Preparing for Waves of Grief

Preparing for waves of grief may be possible by pinpointing ahead of time trigger points we know will make life difficult. If we know a certain trigger point is inevitable, we may schedule more quiet time for retrospection and not expect as much out of ourselves as we deal with the trauma of the wave; however, it is important that we maintain some semblance of normalcy and busyness if at all possible.

When we are caught off guard by a wave of grief, it may be necessary to lower our expectations — change our plans to accommodate the grief process. Knowing ahead of time that waves will come when we least expect them and having a plan in place for those times may lessen the trauma.

Finding Someone to Confide In

It is often helpful to find someone to confide in — someone we trust — someone we believe will understand and not judge us for our vulnerability to the pain caused by the monster called Grief. If we tell them about the trigger point and express the pain, we may feel some relief from the emotional onslaught. Finding a private place and giving way to tears may offer some relief. Crying out to God for help in a moment of prayer often causes the Comforter to come rushing our way in a most effective manner.

Differences in Response to Waves of Grief and Stress

Though all may need to find someone to confide in during times of grief, often men and women respond differently. Though grief is a different emotion from stress, stress often accompanies grief as a close companion.

Abraham Lincoln

According to John Gray, author of *Men Are from Mars, Women Are from Venus,* the most remarkable difference between men and women is their response to stress. *Men generally respond by withdrawing, not talking, and focusing on the solution. Women generally respond by not wanting to be alone, talking, and losing their focus momentarily as they involuntarily succumb to a feeling of confusion.*

Men find relief from stress by focusing on finding a solution either by working it out in their own mind or by seeking professional advice. Often they do not seek for this advice from those closest to them. This is confusing to women because *women find relief from stress by talking about the problem,* even if it is done in a haphazard manner while they are in the state of confusion caused by the stress. This conversation is best accepted by those they love the most. Once a lady or girl feels listened to and understood, she begins to feel better. Once she feels her feelings are validated, the stress clears and she prepares to seek a solution. Often women get caught in the confusion point of stress because they are misunderstood by those who try to assist them and who think it will help to force them to concentrate on the solution before their minds are relieved of the confusion and emotions of turmoil caused by the stress. This is impossible for her to do.

A woman intuitively knows how to help another woman during stress points; a man must learn correct responses before he can negotiate this stage. His immediate focus on a solution and her immediate confusion and desire to talk may become a complexity to both, causing Grief to grasp a greater hold and leaving both parties unfulfilled. Learning to understand and negotiate our differences helps us feel less stress and keeps the monster called Grief at bay during difficult times.

Points to Ponder

➤ *Waves of grief often overtake us at the most unexpected moments.*

➤ *Waves of grief are often a response to trigger points.*

➤ *To prepare for waves of grief we learn to anticipate trigger points.*

➤ *Making time in our schedule for grief is an important part of recovery.*

➤ *When we are caught off guard by a wave of grief, it is often necessary to lower our expectations and change our plans.*

➤ *It is important to find someone whom we trust to confide in.*

➤ *Jesus is our chief Comforter.*

➤ *Men and women are both inundated with grief in a similar fashion but Grief's companion, Stress, brings another aspect to contend with.*

➤ *Men and women respond to stress differently.*

➤ *Learning to understand and negotiate our differences helps us feel less stress.*

Prayers

➤ *Jesus, I know I will feel waves of grief at times and it will be difficult to bear.*

➤ *I may be able to see a wave of grief coming if I learn to detect the trigger points in my life. Would You help me?*

➤ *Lord, would You help me to rearrange my schedule so when Grief attacks I will be able to bear it?*

➤ *Thank You for helping me find someone I can trust to confide in. You are the one who supplies all my needs according to Your riches in glory!*

➤ *Jesus, You are my chief Comforter. I am so grateful!*

➤ *Lord, I want to understand the inner workings of grief and stress and the differences between men and women so I will have the tools to understand myself and others.*

➤ *I thank You for helping me learn to understand and negotiate differences so waves of grief do not overwhelm me beyond the point that I can bear.*

"*I have always found that mercy bears richer fruits than strict justice.*"

— *Abraham Lincoln*

Chapter Eight

Avoiding the Issue ~ Stage One

Jesus Heals the Brokenhearted

The first stage of grief, avoiding the issue, is often accompanied by shock. If the loss is sudden and unexpected this stage is different than if the loss is anticipated. Either way, avoiding the issue and shock both play into dealing with loss. In this stage the victim may pretend the loss is not real.

Grief Takes Time

Though this may appear to be futile thinking to someone who has not experienced it, this stage is important in the healing process and should not be rushed through or scorned as unimportant. Recovery from loss takes time and nothing replaces that essential element.

Sharing Happy Memories

When avoiding the issue or supporting someone who is in this early stage of grief, it is often beneficial to talk about the good memories associated with the happy days. Sharing these memories eases the pain.

Someone once said, *"To love is to hurt but not to love is not to live."* If we have loved, we have been blessed with life. If this therapy is successful, and it often is, we may hear laughing and excited voices as happy days are relived and memories are shared.

This is normal and it is a mistake to stifle this reaction to grief. Normal function while we avoid grief softens the entrance into the next stage, anger and fear.

Offering Support during this Stage

It is often counterproductive to give advice concerning the grief process during the denial stage. They are not ready to face it. Forcing them to consider the grief process prematurely ejects them from this first stage into the next stage, which is not so pretty — anger and fear.

Often it helps to spend quality time with the person, making life as easy and enjoyable as possible. Help them to do the simple tasks necessary to face immediate responsibilities of everyday life.

At times the grief-stricken person may want to be left alone. This request should be honored as long as it does not last for long periods of time. Try to protect them from doing something they will regret later. Be available.

Sometimes a hug with no words exchanged brings healing and allows an outlet for grief to vent itself.

To recap in helping a grief victim who is avoiding the issue:

> *Encourage them to talk about good memories of happy days.*

> *Don't offer advice about how they should deal with grief.*

> *Spend quality time with the person.*

> *If they want to be left alone, withdraw but remain available.*

"He has a right to criticize, who has a heart to help."

— *Abraham Lincoln*

Points to Ponder

➤ *Avoiding the issue is often accompanied by shock.*

➤ *Sharing memories from the happy days eases the pain during this stage of grief.*

➤ *To help someone in this stage, share memories, don't offer advice, spend quality time with them, and remain available.*

Prayers

➤ *Jesus, I can't believe this has happened to me. Life was so good before this.*

➤ *Lord, thank You for all of the wonderful times we had. The memories of days gone by will always be a precious treasure.*

Lana Faces Divorce
Story of Real Life Trauma

After eighteen years of marriage Lana became aware something was amiss. As she probed to see if she could decipher it, she became aware of a certain lady in the church her husband pastored who spent a lot of time in his office helping him plan services, texting him, and doing anything else she could do to be near him. Alarm bells went off in Lana's heart and head.

Lana determined to sit down with her husband and reason with him regarding this individual. Surely he, the pastor who carefully guarded sheep, would realize he himself was in danger. Lana waited until she felt it was a good time and then she gingerly approached the subject in what she felt was an appropriate manner. Instead of the grateful introspection she hoped to see, he responded in anger. "What! After all these years you don't trust me!" he stormed.

Within five years the couple was divorced, the husband resigned his church, Lana moved to another state to be close to her family, and the husband was engaged to be married to the woman Lana had warned him about.

Lana had in times past faced the monster called Grief, but this time when the monster arrived he brought with him weapons of mass destruction. The pain lasted long and had many facets, the betrayal felt agonizing, and the far-reaching effects on the church, their sons, and the neighborhood bore elements of shame and disaster Lana had never imagined possible.

"No man is good enough to govern another man without that other's consent."

"My concern is not whether God is on our side; my greatest concern is to be on God's side, for God is always right."

— *Abraham Lincoln*

Chapter Nine

Anger and Fear ~ Stage Two

Jesus Heals the Brokenhearted

Once we face the issue, anger and fear set in because the person is not yet ready to deal with the loss and come to a place of acceptance. When a grieving person feels the helplessness caused by the fact that they cannot change the outcome of a tragic event, they feel angry, fearful or both.

The Flipside of Helplessness

During the anger and fear stage we may feel we have been violated. *Why did this happen? It should have been stopped! It should be stopped but I don't know how to accomplish it. I feel helpless to stop the loss. I am angry. I am afraid.*

The flipside of helplessness is anger. Depending on the temperament of the person, this stage may be overshadowed by fear and insecurity. Often we are rendered helpless by the monster called Grief. This feeling incites anger, fear, and insecurity. This is most prevalent when Grief comes as a result of betrayal, misunderstanding, lies, and separation.

Anger, Fear, and Sin

Anger and fear expend a lot of energy that could be used to right a wrong, but when that energy is accompanied by helplessness the anger or fear turns inward and roars at us in the form of suppressed rage. Only short periods of controlled anger are acceptable.

> *"Be ye angry, and sin not: let not the sun go down upon your wrath" (Ephesians 4:26).*

Controlling Our Spirits

When dealing with the anger and fear stage of grief it is important to control our spirits so we do not experience regret later. For those who endeavor to walk in the Spirit, anger should be controlled and managed so it is disposed of in a godly manner. The Bible teaches when we are slow to anger and rule our spirits we are better than the mighty person who conquers a city.

> *"He that is slow to anger is better than the mighty; and he that ruleth his spirit than he that taketh a city" (Proverbs 16:32).*

When we feel fear, we are apt to make those around us feel as though we do not trust them. Our fear causes problems in our relationships with both God and man.

> *"For God hath not given us the spirit of fear; but of power, and of love, and of a sound mind" (II Timothy 1:7).*

I Feel Like I Am Going Crazy

When dealing with the anger and fear stage it is common to feel as if we are going crazy. We may say, "I don't know what is wrong. I feel like I am going crazy." Flashes of anger or paralyzing fear may cause us to imagine doing destructive behaviors. It is important to exhibit self-control and not do something that will inflict further pain and sorrow.

"Cease from anger, and forsake wrath: fret not thyself in any wise to do evil" (Psalm 37:8).

Expressing Ourselves

Finding a person to express our anger or fear to — someone we feel sure will listen and understand — is an important part of controlling our spirits. Some discussion concerning the anger or fear is in order and a feeling of permission granted from those close by or in authority. This permission and understanding go a long way in helping us decipher our feelings and move on to the next stage.

If we suppress or pretend anger or fear does not exist, the power of the rage will affect our mental, physical, and emotional health. It may be important to find a professional Christian counselor to lead us through the process of expressing and disposing of our feelings properly.

Redirected Anger or Fear

The anger, fear, or suppressed rage may involuntarily redirect itself and the person grieving may lash out at persons who are totally uninvolved or even at inanimate objects. They may cower in fear and then lash out in anger intermittently. Some temperaments generally respond to crisis with fear and others with anger.

Constructive redirection of anger or fear may include exercise, playing a competitive game, or becoming involved in a time-consuming or difficult project. Redirecting anger or fear should not include subjecting ourselves to a stressful environment.

Supporting Others

In order to support a person during the anger and fear stage it is important not to take offense. Taking offense and personalizing their actions and feelings may only complicate the healing process. This takes self-control as it is a huge temptation to take it personally when someone lashes out at us with angry words or cowers in fear as though we could not be trusted.

Both of the stages, avoiding the issue and anger and fear, carry certain elements of being out of touch with reality. This is a normal part of grieving and whether we deal with it in ourselves or others it should not be scorned as "wrong" or "bad."

To recap in helping a grief victim face anger or fear:

> *Keep from personalizing the pain by taking offense.*

> *Encourage them to stay safe and to keep from doing something to bring greater sorrow or pain.*

> *Give them permission to feel angry or fearful — it is normal.*

> *Don't expect them to be completely realistic.*

"When you have got an elephant by the hind legs and he is trying to run away, it's best to let him run."

— Abraham Lincoln

Points to Ponder

➤ *When a grieving person feels the helplessness caused by the fact they cannot change the outcome of a tragic event, they feel angry.*

➤ *The flipside of anger is helplessness, fear, and insecurity.*

➤ *The Bible teaches when we are slow to anger and rule our spirits we are better than the mighty person who conquers a city.*

➤ *We may have feelings that spin out of control during the anger and fear stage of grief, making us feel as though we are going crazy.*

➤ *Finding the right person to confide in may bring some relief.*

➤ *Redirecting our anger or fear in a constructive manner may bring some relief.*

➤ *When helping others with the anger and fear stage, don't personalize their pain; encourage them to stay safe, give them permission to grieve, and don't expect them to be completely realistic.*

Prayers

➢ *Jesus, I feel angry. Why did this have to happen to me? I do not deserve this treatment. Can't we erase all of this tragedy and go back to the way it was before? You can do anything, right?*

➢ *Lord, I once heard it said You can unscramble eggs. I need that kind of power in my life today. I feel helpless. I am afraid of the future. I feel insecure.*

➢ *I am doing my best to control my spirit so I do not engage in any activity that would make me feel regret later. Would You help me, Jesus?*

➢ *Sometimes I'm so mixed up I feel like I am going crazy.*

➢ *I need someone I can trust to confide in. Would You help me find that person and would You bless them for helping me through this terrible struggle?*

➢ *Lord, I need to find constructive ways to redirect this anger or fear. What can I do?*

➢ *Jesus, I want to remember how uncomfortable this feeling is so in the future when others are suffering I can be a help to them.*

Edith Faces Prejudice

Story of Real Life Trauma

Edith's world swirled about her as she exhausted her mind by reviewing the events of her day over and over and over. "How could they think such a thing?" she muttered. "Why do they believe that because I don't look just like them I am not valuable?"

Edith reached for her phone and dialed a trusted friend. "Hannah?"

"Yes, Edith! How are you? You sound like something is wrong. What's up?"

Edith's voice trembled as the words tumbled over one another. Hannah listened carefully, understanding that the stress tormenting her dear friend made it difficult for her to make sense. Hannah knew once Edith felt listened to and cared for, her thinking would clear and she would feel better. Hannah encouraged Edith to explain the details by using a list of encouraging words like, "Really? Hmmm. Oh my! Unbelievable! I feel so bad. I'm sorry this happened. I know this must really hurt. What else?"

Once all of the details had been unloaded, Hannah recapped and asked a few questions to make sure she had gotten the picture. Edith's rambling, broken sentences charged with emotion had left a few unanswered questions.

The monster called Grief had visited Edith in the form of prejudice. She felt angry, helpless, and had a desire to retaliate. Hannah's listening ear helped ease the pain.

Chapter Ten

Negotiating for a Change ~ Stage Three

Jesus Heals the Brokenhearted

When it becomes clear to the victim of the monster called Grief that anger and fear is not working to alleviate the recovery process, he or she may switch to the next stage—negotiating for a change. The unreasonable element detected in the previous two stages is part of this stage also as the griever attempts to regain control of the situation through negotiating with God, themselves, or others.

The person grieving is not ready to face the fact that the loss is permanent. They explore all options that may recover their loss in hopes of reversing the damage.

The Blame Game

A person may have a tendency to blame themselves or others for the loss. They say words like, "If only I had . . ." We may nickname this stage the "if onlys." We run the details by a million times and add, "If only . . ."

Or we may ask ourselves again and again, "How did this happen? What could I have done to stop it? Why didn't I see it coming? Why did he or she do that?" and a host of other similar questions.

Shame

Guilt, shame, and regret play a large part in whether this stage sets in for a long season or becomes a fleeting, almost imperceptible moment. Shame is difficult to decipher. We may ask, "Am I guilty of something that caused this terrible thing to happen?" If we are guilty and the evidence is substantiated, the shame may be almost unbearable. Not only do we have the tragedy to bear but we feel it is our fault. It is important to accept the blame, repent, do whatever is necessary to make restitution, and then forgive ourselves and move on.

Working to Keep from Getting Stuck

Many times recovery is based on how the person grieving responds during this stage. It is helpful to talk the "if onlys" out with a trusted friend or counselor. Sometimes writing the "if onlys" out on paper and then rereading them is therapeutic.

Writing a letter to those you wish you could explain your side of the issue to with the intention of destroying the letter after writing it may help ease the pain. We ask the question, "If I could go to anyone involved and say whatever I wanted to say, what would it be?" Once we pinpoint what we would say and write it down, we may feel better.

Supporting Others

In order to support a person during the negotiating for a change stage it is important not to force them into facing the cold, hard reality of the loss but allow them to explore all options available even if they seem ridiculous, simplistic, or immature. Time, patience, honesty, truthfulness, mercy, forgiveness, and love go a long way in helping a person dealing with this stage.

Points to Ponder

➤ During this stage, the grieving person explores all options as they try to recover their loss in hopes of reversing the damage.

➤ The grieving person tries to establish blame.

➤ Guilt, shame, and regret play a large part in whether this stage sets in for a long season or becomes a fleeting, almost imperceptible moment.

➤ It is helpful to write journals or letters to keep from getting stuck.

➤ Time, patience, honesty, truthfulness, mercy, forgiveness, and love go a long way in helping a person dealing with the negotiating for a change stage of grief.

Prayers

➤ Jesus, I am not sure I understand what is going on. I feel so lost. What could I have done to keep this from happening?

➤ Lord, I am not sure if I am guilty of doing something sinful. I am sorry for _____ and ask that Your blood cover any sinful act. I need Your mercy and forgiveness.

➤ Thank You for the blood of Jesus Christ that cleanses us from all sin. I am so grateful to You for making the supreme sacrifice for my sin.

> *I want to make it through this ordeal as quickly as possible. I know it takes time to heal. Would You speed up the process? Would You help me not to get stuck in this stage? I want to be free of this pain.*

> *Jesus, would You help me remember this pain so when others suffer I can help them with patience, honesty, truthfulness, mercy, forgiveness, and love?*

Alex Loses His Parents

Story of Real Life Trauma

Ring! Ringgg! Ringgg! Alex reached for his phone to silence the ringer as he glanced at the caller ID. Hmmm, his brother Bob. "Hello, Bob? What's going on? What! It's Mom? She's had a stroke? Intensive care? Oh my! I will catch the next plane and be right there!"

Alex flipped open his laptop and typed in the URL for his bank account. He had to go see his mother. He knew she wasn't in good health when this happened and wondered if she would live through this. He hoped he could get there in time. How much money was this going to cost? Oh my! So many things to take care of before I can go. Just one phone call can change so much! "Mom, hang in there. I love you, Mom!" he muttered with tears springing to his eyes and a lump gathering in his throat.

After three weeks of sitting beside his mother in intensive care and spending time with his siblings at the home place Alex felt exhausted. He valued the moments when his mother responded to the hymns being sung around the bedside, and though she could not speak or join in because of the damage from the stroke, her eyes spoke volumes and Alex could hear her singing along with them in his mind's ear. She had sung the songs of Zion while she worked as long as Alex could remember. All of her children had her favorite hymns memorized.

Alex returned home to take care of his responsibilities but knew his dear mother was not long for this world. When the call came he was ready and arrived a few hours before she passed on into eternity. "Bye, Mother! I love you!" Alex whispered as she took her final breath and her children continued singing the hymn "'Tis So Sweet to Trust in Jesus." As the days passed, Alex felt as though the very foundation of who He was had been clipped at the source. The loss of his mother was so difficult to bear!

★ Six months later Alex's father followed his wife in death. Alex turned to his brother at the funeral. "You know, Bob? I think Dad grieved himself to death. We tried to keep him happy and busy but he missed Mom so much. They were married so long he just couldn't live without her." ★

"We should be too big to take offense and too noble to give it."

— Abraham Lincoln

Chapter Eleven

Depression and Discouragement
~ Stage Four
Jesus Heals the Brokenhearted

Once all the options have been explored and it becomes clear the loss is permanent, a person feels such hopelessness and despair that it catapults him or her into the fourth stage of grief—depression. This is different from the helplessness they felt during the anger stage. In this stage the griever feels as if there is nothing bright in the future. It feels as though he will never really live again.

My Life Is Ruined

During this stage of depression and discouragement we realize no amount of energy or negotiating will change the fact of the loss. We hurt. It is so uncomfortable. We feel like our life is ruined. All our hopes and dreams are dashed. We feel alone, forsaken, and forgotten. We feel like it will always be this way.

This is a real feeling not to be minimized by self or others. We may struggle to take care of ourselves. It may be difficult to get proper rest and eat nourishing food. We may accidentally miss deadlines or meetings. We may feel like sleeping a long time because we don't feel as if there is any reason to get up. We may feel as if it is hopeless to dress up and mingle with other people. We may feel as though we don't deserve to be taken care of even in simple areas like turning on the heat when it is cold, or the air conditioning when it is hot. These feelings are real and tangible, and they must be embraced and dealt with.

Though this is a stage that finally passes if we continue fighting, when we are struggling with it we feel as though it will never change. It takes determination to face depression in a positive manner. It feels like it will be counterproductive. We may ask ourselves, "What good will it do?" or "Who cares?" Knowing these feelings are normal may help.

We may help others by spending time with the person allowing them to face the cold, hard realities with as many comforts as possible. We may help them with regular responsibilities that may have become cumbersome and difficult because of the energy given to the grief process. This assistance may keep the person from giving up entirely.

Rejoice in Hope

Though during depression and discouragement it may be difficult to maintain a grip on hope, it is essential to existence itself. Hope is the foundation for life and leads us to greater joys as it blossoms into faith and joy. When we find we have nothing else to rejoice about we rejoice in hope.

"Therefore being justified by faith, we have peace with God through our Lord Jesus Christ: by whom also we have access by faith into this

grace wherein we stand, and rejoice in hope of the glory of God" (Romans 5:1-2).

We hope for better days. We hope we will finally be delivered from the monster called Grief and spend happier days when he is gone for good and we come home to find a place filled again with peace and happiness. We have hope that once the monster has been kicked out for good we will be stronger and wiser on the inside where it counts the most. We have hope of life in Heaven with Jesus forever.

> *"And not only so, but we glory in tribulations also: knowing that tribulation worketh patience; and patience, experience; and experience, hope: and hope maketh not ashamed; because the love of God is shed abroad in our hearts by the Holy Ghost which is given unto us" (Romans 5:3-5).*

Saturating Our Lives with Scripture

Reading, memorizing, or listening to audio of the Bible, or anointed preaching is often therapeutic as we struggle to control the mind. As we work to throw off depression and discouragement and find hope for a brighter future the discipline of concentrating on the power of the Word of God powerfully aids our progress. The Book of Psalms is full of encouraging phrases to help focus our thinking on the Lord and deflect difficulty. Saturating our lives with Scripture may prove to be one of the best ways to overcome depression.

> *"The steps of a good man are ordered by the LORD: and he delighteth in his way. Though he*

fall, he shall not be utterly cast down: for the
LORD upholdeth him with his hand. I have been
young, and now am old; yet have I not seen the
righteous forsaken, nor his seed begging bread"
(Psalm 37:23-25).

Maintaining a Routine

Routine is often helpful as it keeps us from
sleeping too much or engaging in unhealthy activities.
If we go to work and church regularly, we may find
this demand is a blessing. It gives us something
constructive to do with our time. It helps us keep
going. If we eat meals and go to bed at regular times it
helps us feel better physically and gives us strength to
fight depression.

David Encouraged Himself

During the years Saul set out to kill David
and David consistently ran from him, the Amalekites
invaded Ziklag where David and his men lived with
their families. While David and his men fought another
battle the enemy burned their city and captured all
their wives and children. David's men were stricken
with grief. They had looked to David for leadership
and felt he had let them down. First they wept and
then they lashed out at David whom they felt was at
fault. In an angry rage they even threatened to stone
him. Instead of retaliating, David encouraged himself
in the Lord.

"Then David and the people that were with him
lifted up their voice and wept, until they had no
more power to weep. And David's two wives were
taken captives, Ahinoam the Jezreelitess, and

Abigail the wife of Nabal the Carmelite. And David was greatly distressed; for the people spake of stoning him, because the soul of all the people was grieved, every man for his sons and for his daughters: but David encouraged himself in the LORD his God" (I Samuel 30:4-6).

David called the priest and began to pray. He asked God for answers to his perplexing questions. "God, should we go after them? Will it do any good?" God responded in the affirmative, offering comfort to David and reassuring him he would recover all he had lost.

"And David recovered all that the Amalekites had carried away: and David rescued his two wives. And there was nothing lacking to them, neither small nor great, neither sons nor daughters, neither spoil, nor any thing that they had taken to them: David recovered all" (I Samuel 30:18-19).

Job—though He Slay Me

Satan gained permission to afflict Job because he felt sure when the hedge God kept around Job was removed, Job would curse God and turn his back on Him. However, Job defeated Satan. God's confidence in Job was not in vain. When the worst of trials faced him, Job declared allegiance to God.

"Though he slay me, yet will I trust in him: but I will maintain mine own ways before him" (Job 13:15).

Elijah Confronts the Heathen Gods

Elijah had faced and conquered possibly the most challenging events of his ministry when he confronted the heathen gods the children of Israel had begun to worship. God answered by fire convincing the people that the God of Elijah was the one true God.

> *"Then the fire of the LORD fell, and consumed the burnt sacrifice, and the wood, and the stones, and the dust, and licked up the water that was in the trench. And when all the people saw it, they fell on their faces: and they said, The LORD, he is the God; the LORD, he is the God" (I Kings 18:38-39).*

Elijah rallied the forces of the people and with their help killed all the prophets of the evil god Baal.

> *"And Elijah said unto them, Take the prophets of Baal; let not one of them escape. And they took them: and Elijah brought them down to the brook Kishon, and slew them there" (I Kings 18:40).*

Elijah Outruns the Chariot

Then Elijah prophesied the drought was over and rain would soon fall. He commanded King Ahab to call for his chariot and race home to beat the storm. God gave Elijah amazing and miraculous strength as he ran before the chariot of Ahab.

> *"And it came to pass in the mean while, that the heaven was black with clouds and wind, and there was a great rain. And Ahab rode,*

*and went to Jezreel. And the hand of the LORD
was on Elijah; and he girded up his loins, and
ran before Ahab to the entrance of Jezreel" (I
Kings 18:45-46).*

Jezebel Threatens to Kill Elijah

After these miraculous victories in Elijah's
ministry King Ahab went to the palace and told his
wife Jezebel all Elijah had done and how he had slain
the prophets of Baal. She became very angry and
promised to kill Elijah.

*"And Ahab told Jezebel all that Elijah had
done, and withal how he had slain all the
prophets with the sword. Then Jezebel sent a
messenger unto Elijah, saying, So let the gods
do to me, and more also, if I make not thy life
as the life of one of them by to morrow about
this time" (I Kings 19:1-2).*

Elijah Loses hope

It seems just when Elijah thought his ministry
had reached new dimensions, he faced death threats.
He lost hope God could deliver him and fled into the
wilderness. He sat under a juniper tree and requested
that God allow him to die there instead of being
delivered into the hand of the queen.

*"But he himself went a day's journey into the
wilderness, and came and sat down under a
juniper tree: and he requested for himself that
he might die; and said, It is enough; now, O
LORD, take away my life; for I am not better
than my fathers" (I Kings 19:4).*

God Responds to Elijah's Depression

God's response to Elijah's depression is encouraging. He sent an angel to minister to Elijah. The angel woke him and fed him; he went back to sleep and the angel woke him and fed him again. The food the angel brought gave him strength for the next forty days!

> *"And the angel of the LORD came again the second time, and touched him, and said, Arise and eat; because the journey is too great for thee. And he arose, and did eat and drink, and went in the strength of that meat forty days and forty nights unto Horeb the mount of God"* (I Kings 19:7-8).

Once Elijah received strength, God spoke and said in essence, "Elijah, what are you doing here in this cave? I have much more work for you to do." After the Lord had given Elijah specific instructions, He sent Elisha to become a part of Elijah's ministry to help him in all he did.

> *"Then he arose, and went after Elijah, and ministered unto him"* (I Kings 19:21).

God did not chide Elijah when he became discouraged and depressed but sent an angel to minister to him, spoke encouraging words, gave him specific instructions, and then sent Elisha to minister to and assist him for the rest of his days.

The Devil Possessed Girl

When Paul and Silas ministered in Macedonia they met a wonderful, godly lady named Lydia. She invited them to stay with her family while they were in the area.

> *"And when she was baptized, and her household, she besought us, saying, If ye have judged me to be faithful to the Lord, come into my house, and abide there. And she constrained us" (Acts 16:15).*

While there they encountered a devil possessed girl. Her masters used her to make money. When she saw Paul and Silas she followed them crying out, *"These men are the servants of the most high God, which shew unto us the way of salvation"* (Acts 16:17).

Day after day she followed them and cried these words. Finally Paul was grieved with her and turning, commanded the evil spirit to depart.

> *"And this did she many days. But Paul, being grieved, turned and said to the spirit, I command thee in the name of Jesus Christ to come out of her. And he came out the same hour" (Acts 16:18).*

The Girl's Masters Become Angry

When the girl's masters realized what had happened they felt angry and upset. If she no longer had the evil spirit but functioned normally they could no longer use her to make money. They dragged Paul and Silas into the marketplace and presented them to the magistrates. They lied to the rulers as they accused them.

> *"And when her masters saw that the hope of their gains was gone, they caught Paul and Silas, and drew them into the marketplace unto the rulers, and brought them to the magistrates, saying, These men, being Jews, do exceedingly trouble our city"* (Acts 16:19-20).

Paul and Silas Are Put in Prison

They riled up the multitude against them until the leadership felt it necessary to punish them in some way to calm the riot. They ordered them to be beaten and thrown in prison. The magistrates charged the jailer to make sure the troublemakers remained safely in jail. When the jailer heard the command he took extra precautions to make sure the prisoners remained secure. He placed them in the inner prison and put their feet in stocks so they could not walk around. Thus feeling secure, the jailer rested.

> *"And when they had laid many stripes upon them, they cast them into prison, charging the jailor to keep them safely: who, having received such a charge, thrust them into the inner prison, and made their feet fast in the stocks"* (Acts 16:23-24).

Paul and Silas Choose to Worship

This imprisonment made life look pretty bleak for Paul and Silas. They had no idea how long they would be there. As they discussed it late that night they chose to rejoice in the Lord. At midnight they began to pray, sing, and offer praise to God. The other prisoners heard them and marveled. As they sang, God sent a great earthquake. The earthquake shook the prison house and miraculously loosed every prisoner's bands! It shook the doors open so they were all free to escape!

> *"And at midnight Paul and Silas prayed, and sang praises unto God: and the prisoners heard them. And suddenly there was a great earthquake, so that the foundations of the prison were shaken: and immediately all the doors were opened, and every one's bands were loosed" (Acts 16:25-26).*

The Jailer Panics

When the jailer woke up, looked out the window, and saw the prison doors open he panicked. He knew it would be his life for theirs if they escaped. He saw no other option at that moment but to kill himself. As the jailer prepared to take his life, Paul cried out with a loud voice, *"Do thyself no harm: for we are all here!"*

> *"And the keeper of the prison awaking out of his sleep, and seeing the prison doors open, he drew out his sword, and would have killed himself, supposing that the prisoners had been fled. But Paul cried with a loud voice, saying, Do thyself no harm: for we are all here" (Acts 16:27-28).*

"Sirs, What Must I Do to Be Saved?"

When the jailer realized the preachers he jailed did not escape at their first chance he brought them into his house. He fell down at their feet, confessing his desire to be saved, *"Sirs, what must I do to be saved?"* He washed their stripes doing all he could to make them comfortable. Then they took him and baptized him and his household.

> *"Then he called for a light, and sprang in, and came trembling, and fell down before Paul and Silas, and brought them out, and said, Sirs, what must I do to be saved? (Acts 16:29-30).*

None of this would have occurred if Paul and Silas had not chosen to rejoice in the Lord during a very dark hour in their lives. As they sat in prison, feet locked in stocks, backs bleeding with open wounds, lied about, and misunderstood by leadership they could have chosen to feel sorry for themselves. Any one of us would have understood if they had chosen an easier path.

Angels Are Ministering Spirits

During times of grief and sorrow we can expect the miraculous. God and His angels are explicitly intertwined. They cannot be separated. When God prepares to do something for His people, He sends angels or saints or both to minister. It is our privilege to be the recipient of such a glorious plan!

"Are they not all ministering spirits, sent forth to minister for them who shall be heirs of salvation?" (Hebrews 1:14)

God Specializes in Impossibilities

As we can ascertain from review of some of these favorite Bible stories, God specializes in impossibilities. There is no impossibility too great for our God. One preacher used the following analogy to help us understand this concept: "God can unscramble eggs!"

During the depression stage of grief it is hardest to believe we have a bright future. Though we submit to the feeling that comes when depression visits, we do not allow ourselves to become comfortable or entrenched with these feelings. Instead, we reach for a better tomorrow trusting God to bring us out of this stage into the final stage—acceptance and redefining reality. It may take courage to face the future and see it as brighter. ***Courage is facing fear with hope.*** Hope is our greatest asset, especially as we battle depression.

Points to Ponder

➢ *When we realize our losses are permanent we enter the depression and discouragement stage of grief.*

➢ *Spending time with a person during the depression and discouragement stage is often helpful.*

➢ *Maintaining a grip on hope is essential to life*

itself. Scripture encourages us to rejoice in hope.

➤ Bible reading, memorization, and anointed preaching help us sharpen our focus on positive things.

➤ David encouraged himself when his men wanted to stone him.

➤ Job maintained integrity with God even though he was faced with large doses of grief.

➤ When Elijah was faced with grief, God sent an angel to minister to him twice and then Elisha to minister to him continually.

➤ When Paul and Silas sang and praised God during a terrible bout with grief, God sent an earthquake to deliver them from prison.

➤ When a child of God is hurting, God sends saints or angels or both to minister to them.

➤ God specializes in impossibilities.

➤ When we believe God does miracles, it is easier for us to trust we have a bright future even when life is difficult.

Prayers

➤ Lord, I know I cannot change this tragedy. Would You help me as I face this reality?

➤ Jesus, it is so difficult to face this stage— depression and discouragement. I want to feel the joy You alone can give. I will rejoice in the hope that someday life will be easier.

➢ *I will do my best to memorize a verse of Scripture today and listen to an anointed sermon so my focus will be on You, Jesus, instead of on my problems.*

➢ *When I think of David and how he chose to encourage himself in You, Lord, even when the men wanted to stone him, I have courage to face my own tragedy with faith.*

➢ *Job maintained his integrity with God even when faced with incredible losses. Lord, I am determined to maintain my integrity with you as well.*

➢ *Wow! When I think of all You did for Elijah it gives me courage to believe You will help me through this terrible problem.*

➢ *Jesus, just as Paul and Silas sang and rejoiced through difficult times, I will sing and praise as well.*

➢ *God, thank You for the saints who reach out to help in time of need. Thank You for sending angels, ministering spirits, to minister to me when I need extra help.*

➢ *I know You specialize in impossibilities. I have one I need Your help with.*

➢ *Jesus, I believe someday I will be free of the pain I suffer today. I believe You have a bright future for me.*

*"In this sad world of ours, sorrow comes to all;
and, to the young, it comes with bitterest agony,
because it takes them unawares."*

— *Abraham Lincoln*

Janine Faces Rejection and Misunderstanding

Story of Real Life Trauma

"Uncle Darrell? This is Janine. I haven't talked to you for a long time—ever since I was a teenager and moved out of state. I hope you don't mind, but I need some advice. I know I can trust you."

"Yes, Janine! So nice to hear your voice! I was just asking your mother about you the other day. What's on your mind?"

"Well it was my mother who encouraged me to confide in you, Uncle Darrell. The church I am going to is nothing like the one you and I grew up in back home. And now . . ." Janine trailed off as her voice choked.

"What is it, Janine.?" Uncle Darrell probed.

"Well, there has been a terrible misunderstanding. Someone told a lie about me to the pastor here and he believes it. Without even giving me a chance to defend myself, he has taken action against me. He has taken my class, I have been asked to step down from the choir, and I no longer have a bus route. I just don't get it! Why did he believe that other person without even listening to my side.? He is so sure the other person is telling the truth that when I tried to tell him my side of things he accused me of lying. I just can't stand it and I don't know what to do. I feel embarrassed in front of all my friends and associates. I feel misunderstood and the cruelty of all of it is almost more than I can bear."

"Well, first of all, Janine, remember this is not God's fault. Don't allow your heart to become bitter toward God. Even if your pastor is wrong, you cannot allow that misunderstanding to come between you and God. Does that make sense.?"

"Yes, it does, Uncle Darrell. I will make sure I keep praying and will do my best to keep my heart right with God. In the meantime, I think I need to look for a different church. Would you pray with me.?"

Nowhere Else to Go by Nathan Greene

*"The fiery trials through which we pass
will light us down in honour or dishonour
to the latest generation."*

— *Abraham Lincoln*

Chapter Twelve

Acceptance and Redefining Reality ~ Stage Five

Jesus Heals the Brokenhearted

The last and final stage of grief—acceptance and redefining reality—comes when the victim understands no amount of negotiating or giving up will help. The reality of the tragedy is permanent. It is no longer possible to live according to the previous paradigm. New options must be explored and conquered.

Memories Become Precious Nuggets

We begin to let go of the painful memories and once again may resort to the memories enjoyed during the first stage of grief—avoiding the issue. But this time the memories are precious nuggets to be treasured as something that can never be revisited, while during the time we avoided the issue it is almost as if the loss is annulled during the visitation of pleasant memories.

The Miracle of Hope

God gave Abraham and Sarah the promise of a son. They hoped it would come true. After they became old and it seemed that even hope was fruitless they continued to hope. God performed a miracle and they received the promised child. From this child many nations were formed.

> *"Who against hope believed in hope, that he might become the father of many nations, according to that which was spoken, So shall thy seed be" (Romans 4:18).*

During acceptance we realize a glimmer of hope shining through the darkness. The light, though far away, shines brighter than any light we have ever seen. It is difficult to believe the miracle of such a light lies in our paths. We hope for a bright future. We accept the loss and begin to build new relationships and dream new dreams.

Redefining Reality

Once we accept the loss and begin to rebuild we are faced with defining a new reality. Our past experiences both good and bad become part of our redefinition. If we learn from our mistakes and our tragedies and we capture the joy of our previous good, we often end up with a brighter future than the life we lived before the monster called Grief visited.

Worldwide evangelist Lee Stoneking often says, *"Make the devil wish he had never messed with you!"* By gathering all our resources, including the bad experiences we encountered, and using them to redefine our future we can defeat the enemy.

Scripture promises all things work together for good to them who love the Lord. This doesn't mean life is a bed of roses, but it does mean if we effectually combine our experiences we will redefine a new reality in a positive sense.

"And we know that all things work together for good to them that love God, to them who are the called according to his purpose" (Romans 8:28).

Adjusting to a New Reality

This stage of acceptance also takes time as we continue to adjust to our new reality. It may even seem as if we need to reacquaint ourselves with the person inside.

After suffering the sudden loss of a close friend, Robert L. Veninga, while writing a book to help others with similar loss, explains his findings:

> *I visited physicians and psychologists, nurses and chaplains. I asked them what they had learned in helping people through difficult crises.*
>
> *They were agreed on two points: First, most everyone is changed by crisis. Second, most people do in fact survive. And often they survive with a new purpose and a new direction. As a psychologist said: 'Sometimes the new life is better than the old.'* (A Gift of Hope: How We Survive Our Tragedies, *Robert L. Veninga, 1985, p. 3).*

Supporting a Person during This Stage

To support a person during the acceptance and redefining reality stage of grief, offer encouraging and admiring words to let them know you too accept their new reality and you still value and care for them.

Kicking Out the Monster and Locking the Door

During this final stage of grief we no longer fear the monster called Grief. We boldly look him in the eye and say, "Grief, you are not welcome in this house! Get out!" Then as he slinks away we shut and lock the door, hoping we never have to deal with him again.

Points to Ponder

➢ *The last stage of grief begins when we accept the fact the loss is permanent and begin to face a new reality.*

➢ *Memories become nuggets to revisit and treasure.*

➢ *We see glimmers of hope and believe in a brighter future.*

➢ *We begin to combine all our experiences to date and define a new reality.*

➢ *We begin to adjust to a new reality.*

➢ *To help others, we express our acceptance of*

> *their new reality and let them know they are valuable and cared for.*

> *During the acceptance stage of grief, we kick the monster called Grief out and lock the door.*

Prayers

> *Jesus, I have been through a very difficult time in my life. I realize life will never be the same as it once was but I am still in the palm of Your hand. I will go wherever You lead me.*

> *Lord, the precious memories of days gone by have become treasures to keep and revisit from time to time. I thank You for these valuable nuggets.*

> *I am struggling to define a new reality in my life. I want to do it in a way that pleases You, Jesus, a way that is founded on the Word of God.*

> *I believe You have a great plan and I am excited about it. I will follow You the rest of my days.*

> *Slowly I am adjusting to the new life You have provided. It will take time. I appreciate Your help every step of the way.*

> *Jesus, I know from time to time Grief visits all of us. I don't like it when he comes to my house. Today I have kicked him out, shut the door, and locked it. Thank You for bringing me to this day of victory!*

Maggie Finds out She Was Adopted

Story of Real Life Trauma

Maggie's life crashed down around her as she heard the words and then repeated them over and over. "You were adopted."

"Adopted? Rejected and abandoned by my own parents? Why?" Maggie muttered, more to herself than to the parents who sat on the chair before her—people she had always believed were her real parents! She felt dumbfounded. She had always had this nagging feeling that she didn't fit in this family—now she understood why. "Why didn't they tell me sooner? Who am I anyway?" Maggie asked herself. "And where did I come from?" A flood of other questions crowded her mind.

It took some time before Maggie accepted the fact that though she may have been rejected and abandoned by her birth parents, she was chosen by her adoptive parents. It is a privilege to be chosen.

"But when the fulness of the time was come, God sent forth his Son, made of a woman, made under the law, to redeem them that were under the law, that we might receive the adoption of sons. And because ye are sons, God hath sent forth the Spirit of his Son into your hearts, crying, Abba, Father. Wherefore thou art no more a servant, but a son; and if a son, then an heir of God through Christ" (Galatians 4:4-7).

"Many people will walk in and out of your life, but only true friends will leave footprints in your heart."

— Eleanor Roosevelt

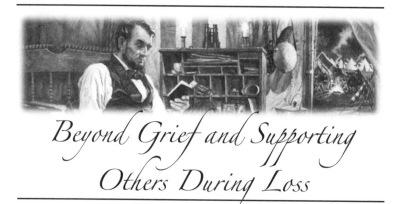

Beyond Grief and Supporting Others During Loss

- Green Pastures of Forgiveness
- The Joy of Grief
- The Comforter
- Suffering Turns into Compassion
- Learning to Say the Right Words

"To err is human; to forgive, divine."

— *Alexander Pope*

Chapter Thirteen

Green Pastures of Forgiveness

Jesus Heals the Brokenhearted

Finding a Peaceful New Reality

In order for us to maintain integrity with God and find a new reality that lets go of loss but does not include bitterness, hardness of heart or resentment, we must forgive. During the acceptance and redefining reality stage of grief it is necessary to consciously work to maintain a clean heart free of debilitating works of the flesh. We submit to the will of God and forgive unconditionally as He forgave us.

"To be wronged is nothing, unless you continue to remember it."

— Confucius

Repentance, Reconciliation, and Forgiveness

As we seek to bring clarity to the term *forgiveness* we first look at repentance and reconciliation. This helps us clearly define forgiveness.

Repentance is a turning away from sin—a changing of the mind—a determination to live differently in the future than we have in the past. We feel bad about our actions in the past. This sorrow turns into repentance and we find a new life that loves God and hates evil.

> *"For godly sorrow worketh repentance to salvation not to be repented of: but the sorrow of the world worketh death. For behold this selfsame thing, that ye sorrowed after a godly sort, what carefulness it wrought in you, yea, what clearing of yourselves, yea, what indignation, yea, what fear, yea, what vehement desire, yea, what zeal, yea, what revenge! In all things ye have approved yourselves to be clear in this matter"* **(II Corinthians 7:10-11).**

"Forgiveness is the fragrance that the violet sheds on the heel that has crushed it."

— Mark Twain

Reconciliation is doing our best to make up for a wrong we feel convicted about. Reconciliation is what Jesus did for us because He knew we did not have the ability to do it for ourselves. We find holiness only because He is holy and He allows us to put on Christ through reconciling ourselves to Him through the blood of the cross.

> *"And, having made peace through the blood of his cross, by him to reconcile all things unto himself; by him, I say, whether they be things in earth, or things in heaven. And you, that were sometime alienated and enemies in your mind by wicked works, yet now hath he reconciled in the body of his flesh through death, to present you holy and unblameable and unreproveable in his sight" (Colossians 1:20-22).*

"The weak can never forgive. Forgiveness is the attribute of the strong."

— Mahatma Gandhi

Forgiveness is turning away from the desire to punish another for a wrong we feel the effects of. Jesus forgave us and then asked us to do the same for others.

> *"And be ye kind one to another, tenderhearted, forgiving one another, even as God for Christ's sake hath forgiven you" (Ephesians 4:32).*

"To forgive is to set a prisoner free and discover that the prisoner was you."

— *Lewis B. Smedes*

Laying Aside the Desire to Punish

When we forgive, we abandon the desire for revenge. We don't necessarily put ourselves in a position to be hurt by them again. This is not a necessary part of forgiveness. Trust is earned; forgiveness is given unconditionally.

"You will know that forgiveness has begun when you recall those who hurt you and feel the power to wish them well."

— *Lewis B. Smedes*

So Great Salvation!

When repentance, reconciliation, and forgiveness work together, they bring holiness into our lives and we experience what Scripture refers to as "so great salvation"!

"How shall we escape, if we neglect so great salvation; which at the first began to be spoken by the Lord, and was confirmed unto us by them that heard him" (Hebrews 2:3).

"The ability to forgive is one of man's greatest achievements."

— Bryant H. McGill

Look for a Chance to Forgive Today

Someone once admonished, *"Look for a chance to forgive today."* If we live each day with this goal in mind and forgive immediately when we feel the root of bitterness trying to establish itself in our lives, we will be free from the results of pain caused when we refuse to forgive.

"Looking diligently lest any man fail of the grace of God; lest any root of bitterness springing up trouble you, and thereby many be defiled" (Hebrews 12:15).

"Resentment is like drinking poison and then hoping it will kill your enemies."

— Nelson Mandela

God's Forgiveness Is Conditional

Every time we forgive we put ourselves in direct line for God's forgiveness toward us. Forgiveness is one of the most important principles in God's Word.

Those who live with the attitude of "looking for a chance to forgive" are healthier, happier, and have more friends than those who hold grudges and hesitate to forgive. If we are slow to forgive others God is slow to forgive us. This is a scary thought!

> *"For if ye forgive men their trespasses, your heavenly Father will also forgive you: but if ye forgive not men their trespasses, neither will your Father forgive your trespasses" (Matthew 6:14-15).*

"Forgiveness is not about forgetting. It is about letting go of another person's throat."

— *W. Paul Young*

God Covers Our Sin Up
—He Forgets!—

When we ask God to forgive us, He covers our sin with the precious blood of Jesus Christ, and He actually forgets it. We have difficulty with forgetting but God is good at it.

"Thou hast forgiven the iniquity of thy people, thou hast covered all their sin. Selah" (Psalm 85:2).

"One of the keys to happiness is a bad memory."
— *Rita Mae Brown*

Forgiveness Is a Privilege

Forgiveness is a privilege and something we do, not to help another person, but to keep our own hearts pure and right. When we learn to forgive unconditionally we reap the reward of such.

"Forgiveness is a gift you give yourself."
— *Suzanne Somers*

Turn the Other Cheek

It may be easy for us to forgive someone who accidentally steps on our toes, but it takes the grace of God to forgive someone who stomps our foot on purpose! Jesus tried to conceptualize this in the minds of His disciples when He taught them to turn the other cheek when someone slapped them in the face.

"*But I say unto you, That ye resist not evil: but whosoever shall smite thee on thy right cheek, turn to him the other also.*" (*Matthew 5:39*).

"*Forgiveness means it finally becomes unimportant that you hit back.*"

— *Anne Lamott*

Forgiveness from a Financial Standpoint

Forgiveness from a financial standpoint includes reviewing a legitimate debt, then making a decision to release the debtor from responsibility regarding that debt.

Looking at forgiveness from a financial standpoint and then applying the concepts to our relationships helps us to make the right decision when we feel we have been purposely wronged. We review the wrong then release the debtor from any responsibility.

When Jesus gave us *The Lord's Prayer* He included a phrase dealing with debt—He told us to forgive others because He has forgiven us. We are debtors to Him and have a reciprocal responsibility to in turn forgive others.

"And forgive us our debts, as we forgive our debtors" (Matthew 6:12).

"There is no revenge so complete as forgiveness."
— Josh Billings

Building a Bridge of Forgiveness

Forgiveness is not something we do after we've been asked for forgiveness or after we've thought about it and decided whether the transgressor deserves forgiveness or not. Forgiveness is best given unconditionally, from the heart, with no strings attached. The other person's response is their business. When we forgive we build a bridge for ourselves.

"He that cannot forgive others breaks the bridge over which he must pass himself; for every man has need to be forgiven."
— Thomas Fuller

"I will forgive those who criticize me unjustly."

— *Anonymous*

God Doesn't Trade Fairly

If all of us got what we deserved, none of us would be saved, but God doesn't trade fairly. He gives *"beauty for ashes, the oil of joy for mourning, the garment of praise for the spirit of heaviness"* that we *"might be called trees of righteousness, the planting of the LORD, that he might be glorified"* (Isaiah 61:3).

"Always forgive your enemies - nothing annoys them so much."

— *Oscar Wilde*

A Worthy Quote on Forgiveness

Abraham Lincoln has often been attributed as writing this speech on forgiveness; however, it is not a substantiated claim. Nevertheless, it is so well said it is worth repeating again and again.

I will greet this day with a forgiving spirit. For too long, every ounce of forgiveness I owned was locked away, hidden from view, waiting for me to bestow its precious presence upon some worthy person. Alas, I found most people to be singularly unworthy of my valuable forgiveness, and since they never asked for any, I kept it all for myself. Now, the forgiveness that I hoarded has sprouted inside my heart like a crippled seed yielding bitter fruit. No more.

At this moment, my life has taken on new hope and assurance. Of all the world's population, I am one of the few possessors of the secret to dissipating anger and resentment. I now understand that forgiveness has value only when it is given away. By the simple act of granting forgiveness, I release the demons of the past about which I can do nothing, and I create in myself a new heart, a new beginning. I will greet this day with a forgiving spirit. I will forgive even those who do not ask for forgiveness. Many are the times when I have seethed in anger at a word or deed thrown into my life by an unthinking or uncaring person. I have wasted valuable hours imagining revenge or confusion. Now I see the truth revealed about this psychological rock inside my shoe. The rage I nurture is often one-sided, for my offender seldom gives thought to his offense. I will now and forevermore silently offer my forgiveness even to those who do not see that they need it. By the act of forgiving, I am no longer consumed by unproductive thoughts. I give up my bitterness. I am content in my soul and effective again with my fellow man.

I will greet this day with a forgiving spirit. I will forgive those who criticize me unjustly. Knowing that slavery in any form is wrong, I also know that the person who lives a life according to the opinion of others is a slave. I am not a slave. I have chosen my counsel.

I know the difference between right and wrong. I know what is best for the future of my family, and neither misguided opinion nor unjust criticism will alter my course. Those who are critical of my goals and dreams simply do not understand the higher purpose to which I have been called. Therefore, their scorn does not affect my attitude or action. I forgive their lack of vision, and I forge ahead. I now know that criticism is part of the price paid for leaping past mediocrity.

I will greet this day with a forgiving spirit. I will forgive myself. For many years, my greatest enemy has been myself. Every mistake, every miscalculation, every stumble I made has been replayed again and again in my mind. Every broken promise, every day wasted, every goal not reached has compounded the disgust I feel for the lack of achievement in my life.

My dismay has developed a paralyzing grip. When I disappoint myself, I respond with inaction and become more disappointed. I realize today that it is impossible to fight an

enemy living in my head. By forgiving myself,
I erase the doubts, fears, and frustration that
have kept my past in the present. From this
day forward, my history will cease to control
my destiny.

> I have forgiven myself.
> My life has just begun.
> I will forgive even those
> who do not ask for forgiveness.
> I will forgive those who
> criticize me unjustly.
> I will forgive myself.
> I will greet this day
> with a forgiving spirit.

—*Anonymous*

"*Forgiveness has value only when it is given away.*"
— *Anonymous*

In the Darkest Hour by Nathan Greene

Abraham Lincoln and the Soldier

Steve Goodier writes in his book, *Riches of the Heart,* about an incident where President Lincoln forgave a soldier for desertion.

> *During the American Civil War, a young man named Roswell McIntyre was*

drafted into the New York Cavalry. The war was not going well. Soldiers were needed so desperately that he was sent into battle with very little training. Roswell became frightened—he panicked and ran. He was later court-martialed and condemned to be shot for desertion.

McIntyre's mother appealed to President Lincoln. She pleaded that he was young and inexperienced and he needed a second chance. The generals, however, urged the president to enforce discipline. Exceptions, they asserted, would undermine the discipline of an already beleaguered army.

Lincoln thought and prayed. Then he wrote a famous statement. "I have observed," he said, "that it never does a boy much good to shoot him."

He wrote this letter in his own handwriting: "This letter will certify that Roswell McIntyre is to be readmitted into the New York Cavalry. When he serves out his required enlistment, he will be freed of any charges of desertion."

That faded letter, signed by the president, is on display in the Library of Congress. Beside it there is a note, which reads, "This letter was taken from the body of Roswell McIntyre, who died at the battle of Little Five Forks, Virginia."

Meeting of President LINCOLN
and Gen'l GRANT.

"It never does a boy (or anybody else for that matter) much good to shoot him. But you might be surprised at the power of forgiveness."

Points to Ponder

> ➤ Part of recovering from the abuse inflicted by the monster called Grief is learning to forgive.

> ➤ Repentance is to turn from sin; reconciliation is to endeavor to make up for sin; forgiveness is to lay aside the desire to punish for sin.

> ➤ The salvation plan God provides for His people is great!

> ➤ When we live with an attitude of looking for a chance to forgive, we find life to be much more pleasant.

> ➤ If we forgive others, God will forgive us.

> ➤ When we repent, God forgets.

> ➤ Forgiveness is a privilege.

> ➤ Jesus teaches us to turn the other cheek.

> ➤ Looking at forgiveness from a financial standpoint helps us to understand the true meaning of forgiveness.

> ➤ When we forgive, we build a bridge to walk on.

> ➤ When God trades, He does not trade fairly.

> ➤ It is worth taking note of Abraham Lincoln's attitude toward forgiveness.

Prayers

> ➢ *Jesus, I find it difficult to foster a spirit of forgiveness. I have been through so much. Would You help me? I know forgiveness is essential if I am to recover fully from this most recent visit from the monster called Grief.*

> ➢ *I am so grateful for the privilege of repentance.*

> ➢ *Thanks for the reconciliation that comes to us because of the cross and the blood You shed in our place when You suffered there.*

> ➢ *Lord, with Your help I will forgive and lay aside the desire to punish those who have hurt me.*

> ➢ *Jesus, to conceptualize and implement the concept of turning the other cheek I need Your grace. I need Your grace to teach me to do this.*

> ➢ *It is not too hard for me to understand forgiveness of a debt. If I owe a bill and then someone else pays it, I am free from the obligation. Help me to forgive others in the same manner that a financial debt is forgiven.*

> ➢ *I will forgive others to build a bridge for the times I need forgiveness.*

> ➢ *God, You trade beauty for ashes and the oil of joy for the spirit of mourning. Those trades are not what we would normally call fair trades. Thank You, Jesus, for Your amazing love.*

> ➢ *Jesus, I will look for a chance to forgive today.*

➤ *Thank You for the privilege of forgiveness.*

➤ *I want to have a forgiving spirit like Abraham Lincoln had. What an amazing American President he was. I thank You, Lord, for his continued influence in the lives of so many of us. I love You, Jesus!*

"I will greet this day with a forgiving spirit."
— *Anonymous*

Solid Rock

Verse One
My hope is built on nothing less
Than Jesus' blood and righteousness;
I dare not trust the sweetest frame,
But wholly lean on Jesus' name.

Chorus
On Christ, the solid Rock, I stand;
All other ground is sinking sand,
All other ground is sinking sand.

Verse Two
When darkness veils His lovely face,
I rest on His unchanging grace;
In every high and stormy gale,
My anchor holds within the veil.

Verse Three
His oath, His covenant, His blood
Support me in the whelming flood;
When all around my soul gives way,
He then is all my hope and stay.

Verse Four
When He shall come with trumpet sound,
Oh, may I then in Him be found;
Dressed in His righteousness alone,
Faultless to stand before the throne.

—William Bradbury, 1863

Marcus Goes to Jail

Story of Real Life Trauma

Marjorie heard alarm bells go off in her spirit as she peeked out the kitchen window after hearing a car in the driveway and saw two county sheriffs' cars. "What's going on? It is only 5:00 AM," she muttered to herself. She watched as they climbed out of their vehicles and headed for the front door. Marjorie pulled her robe closer and hurried to the door. The dog barked a warning followed by a threatening growl as a loud knock sounded. Marjorie spoke calming words to the dog as she grasped his collar and opened the door.

"Yes," she breathed, "may I help you?"

"Is Marcus home?" one of the officers asked in a kind but firm voice.

"Yes, he is asleep upstairs. Is something wrong?" Marjorie answered with a trembling tone.

"Would you let him know we are here and ask him to come down to talk with us?" the officer requested.

"Okay. Would you like to come in? I will go wake him up. Just a moment." Marjorie scrambled up the stairs, tears blurring her eyes. What had Marcus done this time?

After a brief interview with the officers, they handcuffed Marcus and took him away in one of the police cars. Marjorie sank into her favorite chair, put her head in her hands, and began to sob. Where did Marcus go wrong? I tried to raise him right. When oh when will this nightmare ever end?

"Laughter and tears are meant to turn the wheels of the same machinery of sensibility; one is wind-power, and the other water-power; that is all."

— Oliver Wendell Holmes

Chapter Fourteen

The Joy of Grief

Jesus Heals the Brokenhearted

When the monster called Grief finally retreats and we have successfully locked the door and placed a guard so he cannot barge in at a moment's notice and catch us unaware, we look back. We may find during the darkest moments of confusion, fear, doubt, anger, and frustration we turned to the One and only One who gives real comfort—the Comforter Himself, Jesus Christ. We realize that during those moments we really began to know Him as our Savior and Lord.

Forever Changed

As we walk away from the trauma, we realize we are not the same person who originally experienced the tragedy. We are changed. If we allowed Jesus to comfort and direct our lives, we are changed for the better. If we became bitter and hardened our heart toward God, we are changed for the worse. In any event we find we are forever and unforgettably altered.

The Secret of the Lord

In this chapter we will look at the lives of those of us who clung to Jesus and allowed Him to change us during trauma. There is joy in knowing Jesus is always there in time of need; He is there in the darkest of nights; He will never leave us nor forsake us; He becomes a part of who we become after the tragedy. Joy shines on our face because we know if the monster called Grief ever visits us again, we will be able to withstand him. Jesus, along with His host of mighty angels, will protect us! It is as if we have learned a little secret that causes us to grasp hold of a deep-seated trust in God at the very core of who we have become.

> *"The secret of the LORD is with them that fear him; and he will shew them his covenant. Mine eyes are ever toward the LORD; for he shall pluck my feet out of the net"* (Psalm 25:14-15).

Forever after this, whenever we know that a friend, loved one, or acquaintance is battling with the monster called Grief, we long to share our secret. Articulating the secret is not always easy but we know if the person will look to Jesus, will allow Him to fight, comfort, and then defeat the enemy, the victory will be won.

> *"But unto you that fear my name shall the Sun of righteousness arise with healing in his wings"* (Malachi 4:2).

Comfort Others
with the Comfort We Felt

We comfort others with the same comfort God provides for us during times of deep sorrow. When we become aware of others' pain we remember our own and do all we can to bring comfort.

> *"Blessed be God, even the Father of our Lord Jesus Christ, the Father of mercies, and the God of all comfort; who comforteth us in all our tribulation, that we may be able to comfort them which are in any trouble, by the comfort wherewith we ourselves are comforted of God. For as the sufferings of Christ abound in us, so our consolation also aboundeth by Christ"* (II Corinthians 1:3-5).

The Joy of the Lord Is Our Strength

The joy of the Lord in our lives gives us strength. When we are fighting with the monster called Grief, he is careful to intimidate us regularly because he knows if we gain the power that comes with the joy of the Lord we will have strength to drive him far from us.

Joy comes from deep within and is the result of knowing the God of the universe is involved in our lives. We have power over the enemy because God is on our side. When we maintain the joy of the Lord in our lives and teach others this key as well, we find the true meaning of living an overcoming life.

> *"Neither be ye sorry; for the joy of the LORD is your strength"* (Nehemiah 8:10).

Points to Ponder

➤ As we look back over the time we battled with the monster called Grief, we realize we were changed by the encounter.

➤ The joy of grief comes when we surrender to God during times of battle with the monster called Grief and come away changed for the better because we did not succumb to bitterness, wrath, and anger.

➤ Once we learn about the secret the righteous possess, we offer comfort to others.

➤ The joy of the Lord is our strength and is used to overcome the enemy and keep him at bay.

Prayers

➤ Jesus, I have been changed by this encounter with the monster called Grief.

➤ Would You help me to rid myself of any wrath, anger, and bitterness so I will be free to enjoy the secret that is with the righteous?

➤ I know You are with me; and You never leave me nor forsake me. I am Your child and You care for me. I am going to be all right.

➤ I feel the comfort of Your precious Spirit washing over me today.

➤ I will do my best to tell others about the comfort You alone can give.

➤ I know the joy of the Lord is my strength. I want to remain strong so I can daily defeat the enemy. Would You help me to maintain the joy of the Lord in my life?

"Let us have faith that right makes might, and in that faith, let us, to the end, dare to do our duty as we understand it."

— *Abraham Lincoln*

"*Friends come and go, but Jesus stays.*"

— *Lee Stoneking*

Chapter Fifteen

The Comforter

Jesus Heals the Brokenhearted

The presence of the Lord is the most comforting factor as we grieve. Friends come and go, but Jesus stays.

"Let your conversation be without covetousness; and be content with such things as ye have: for he hath said, I will never leave thee, nor forsake thee" (Hebrews 13:5).

The Value of an Established Prayer Life

Since Jesus is the best part of our lives, it is important to enter the grief process armed with a good relationship with God. His comfort is almost automatic if we already have an established prayer life that keeps us connected to God and His comforting presence.

There are many reasons to work toward establishing a consistent prayer life while we are young. Knowing we will face monumental decisions during times of great pressure in the future is one of the most important reasons.

When the monster called Grief comes to visit, he disrupts all of our normal activities and insists on changing our schedule. If we have a prayer life built into our lives so completely that we cannot dress and walk out the door without first reading some Scripture and praying, we will find a sustaining holy presence during trauma.

The Pressure of Life's Seasons

Life's seasons bring their own unique challenges. For instance, when we are in school, the homework is grueling and the hours are long. When we are first married, the adjustment is difficult and we are focused on succeeding in making a life together. When we are expecting a child, we feel tired and restless as we prepare for the miracle of life to visit our homes. When we have a new baby, life is definitely disrupted with demands from the little one that seemingly consume every waking hour. When we have toddlers to run after, cook for, clothe, train, and love, the days rush by in a whirl of activity. When the children are in school, we are faced with another rush of activity as we facilitate their education. When we have teenagers, we feel the stress of children in the home who are part adult, part toddler. The conundrum is a challenge. When we face midlife crisis or menopause, life is a constant battle as we struggle to control our spirits.

All through these stages we labor to make enough money to pay the bills and to ease the stress in life. Decisions concerning finances affect all of the other areas of life.

As we face the golden years, the body aches and we have health issues difficult to face and overcome.

We look in the mirror and say, "Who is this person looking back at me? He or she looks like they are getting old." When we lie on our deathbed or spend time in a nursing home, we feel weak, helpless, and unable to make positive change.

Jesus Is the Center of My Life

Life—what is the meaning of all of this? It has real meaning only if Jesus Christ is the center of everything. He knows all, is all powerful, is everywhere at the same time, and He cares about us. He wants to be involved in everything we do in each stage of life and ministry. Only what we do for Him will last.

"If in this life only we have hope in Christ, we are of all men most miserable" (I Corinthians 15:19).

Eternal Life Is Our Goal

Our real goal in this life on earth is eternal life in Heaven. This life is only a test or a time when we have the privilege of relying upon Jesus to lead and guide us through the darkness.

"For now we see through a glass, darkly; but then face to face: now I know in part; but then shall I know even as also I am known" (I Corinthians 13:12).

Jesus Is the Only Answer

When we are visited by the monster called Grief, we are particularly in need of God who is powerful and wise. He knows exactly what we need and is able to take care of us.

If we learn to trust and love Him before the monster called Grief visits us, we have Someone to cling to and to protect us during the time Grief is there.

It Is Never Too Late!

We are never too young or too old to turn to Jesus. In whatever season of life we find ourselves, we can reach to Him on a regular basis. When we allow His presence to wash over us regularly as we make it a daily habit to enter His throne room, we fortify ourselves against the enemy. When Grief comes to visit, he may wreak havoc with our lives but he does not take control—Jesus is stronger and wiser than Grief and He maintains control of our lives.

"We are troubled on every side, yet not distressed; we are perplexed, but not in despair; persecuted, but not forsaken; cast down, but not destroyed; always bearing about in the body the dying of the Lord Jesus, that the life also of Jesus might be made manifest in our body" (II Corinthians 4:8-10).

Making a Commitment

If we find we have not yet made a commitment to daily prayer and Bible reading, let's consider making it a priority to do so today. Jesus is our Comforter and is the only real answer to defeating the monster called Grief who visits us from time to time.

Begin with making a commitment to pray at least 12 minutes every day in connection with dressing the outer man as we prepare for our days. It is actually more important to dress the inner man than it is to dress the outer man. Armed with proper inner garments we will be ready to face the enemy of our soul and defeat him properly no matter what the circumstances dictate.

Accept the challenge and defeat the enemy today!

---

12 Minute Prayer Challenge:

I will pray every day for the next thirty days for at least 12 minutes, and will read at least one chapter in the Bible. I plan to renew that pledge at the end of the thirty days and to do it again and again for the rest of my life.

Signature _____

Points to Ponder

➤ Jesus is our chief Comforter and will never leave us nor forsake us.

➤ If we have an established prayer life when Grief comes to call, we will be equipped to handle his onslaught.

➤ Each of life's seasons has its particular difficulties to overcome.

➤ We strive to make Jesus the center of our lives.

➤ Eternal life is our most important goal.

➤ Jesus Christ is the only real answer for life's dilemmas.

➤ We are never too young or too old to give our lives to Jesus.

➤ It is important to make a strong commitment to consistent prayer.

Prayers

➢ *Jesus, You are the One I run to when I need comfort. You are the best!*

➢ *As I face life's challenges, I am grateful for a habit that includes daily prayer.*

➢ *Lord, I know no season of life is easy. Each season has its own unique difficulties. I will not wait for a more convenient season to make my commitment but will give You all of my life today.*

➢ *Jesus, You are the center of my life!*

➢ *Eternal life with You is my most cherished goal in life.*

➢ *You are the only real answer to life's dilemmas.*

➢ *I am young and though I do not know what tomorrow holds, I will give You all of my days. I love You!*

➢ *I am old and do not have much time left here on earth but I will give you all of my days for as long as I live. I love You!*

➢ *Lord, I have made a strong commitment to pray consistently. I will not skip days. I will pray every day and will do my best to draw closer and closer to You.*

Lance and the Tragic Accident
Story of Real Life Trauma

Lance felt so excited. He and his dad planned to go hunting today! He had hoped and waited for this day to come. His dad was a busy pastor working long hours to build a church; he seldom had leisure time for this type of thing, and Lance felt delighted as he anticipated their day together. "Dad! Is it time to leave yet?"

"Yes, son. Go get in the truck. I'll be right there."

Lance ran out to the truck and jumped in, pulling his backpack and his rifle in with him. His dad was a crack shot and he had been teaching Lance to hunt as well. Lance could hardly wait to get to the woods.

As Lance and his dad made the journey to the place where they felt the best hunting would be, they visited and had sweet fellowship. Pastor Smith felt a great lump rise in his throat. Feelings of gratefulness to God for giving him and his wife this wonderful son rose from deep within. Lance had been adopted into their family at birth and it was the best thing that had ever happened to them besides experiencing the new birth.

Suddenly Pastor Smith's attention was directed to the road as the truck veered. Thoughts flashed through his mind as he realized they must have hit a patch of ice. *I should have* been more careful, he thought. *I knew there was a chance of ice up here. It's colder here than it is down in the valley.* The truck careened out of control and finally left the road, flipping over several times before thudding to a halt.

Pastor Smith immediately began to call out, "Lance! Lance! Are you OK?" He searched the area and finally found Lance with blood gushing out of his mouth and choking him so he could not breathe. Pastor Smith gathered the boy into his arms, turning him so the blood would run out of his mouth and allow him to breathe. "Son! Son! I'm right here! It's going to be OK!" As the anxious pastor held his son yet closer, he realized with horror the boy's head was crushed. Oblivious to the fact that his son's blood was gushing all over him, he held his child yet closer. The blood mingled with the tears that rolled down his cheeks. Before the ambulance arrived, Pastor Smith knew his son was gone. He had died in his arms. He sat there in the ditch holding the boy and sobbing as he prayed, "Dear God, no! No! No! This cannot be!"

WILLIE LINCOLN, THIRD SON OF PRESIDENT LINCOLN.
DIED FEBRUARY 20, 1862, AT THE AGE OF 12.
From a photograph taken by Brady at Washington, shortly
before the death of Willie Lincoln.

"With the fearful strain that is on me night and day, if I did not laugh I should die."

— Abraham Lincoln

Chapter Sixteen

Learning to Say the Right Words

Jesus Heals the Brokenhearted

Often a grieving person is hurt further by those who wish to help the most. This is generally caused by lack of knowledge and experience.

The person grieving does not need to hear a long philosophical speech on why they are grieving or how they should respond to grief but instead they are reaching for and need simple permission to grieve in their own way as they feel most comfortable.

Distancing ourselves from the grieving person is painful because it may translate as abandonment or rejection. We are tempted to do this when we are afraid we may say or do the wrong thing. Saying nothing as we listen to their expressions of pain and/or just offering a sympathetic hug is better than transmitting the feeling to the person that they are being avoided because of their pain.

If we can say the right words in these instances, the rewards are great. Scripture refers to them as "apples of gold in pictures of silver." This terminology is unusual but we may picture a silver bowl or basket full of golden apples sitting on a lovely table. This is easy on the eyes and gives us a feeling of luxury or being cared for. This is the same feeling we get when a loving friend says the right words when we are hurting.

> *"A word fitly spoken is like apples of gold in pictures of silver" (Proverbs 25:11).*

What Words Should We Avoid?

Learning what to say to a grieving person is an art and may be first comprehended by considering phrases that may inflict further pain and understanding why they are interpreted in that manner.

Here are some examples of what not to say:

➤ *"He or she is in a better place."*

- *The person grieving may hear, "You shouldn't grieve because now things are better than they were when you had your loved one here with you."*

➤ *In cases where a long sickness has preceded death, "Well, he's been gone for a long time now anyway."*

- *The person facing the finality of death and feeling the sting may hear, "Why are you still grieving? You knew they were going to die, didn't you?"*

➤ *"Well, these things come to the best of us. It is all part of life."*

- *The person grieving may hear, "What is your problem? Don't you know this is common and everyone faces this?"*

> ➤ *"It will be fine. You will be all right," or "All things work together for good to them who love the Lord."*

- *The person grieving may hear, "Why are you so upset? Everything is going to be OK. Get over it."*

> ➤ *"Listen! You can't feel like this! You need to pull yourself together!"*

- *The person grieving may hear, "Your grief makes me uncomfortable. I don't want to be bothered with it."*

> ➤ *"Let's see. How can we get you past this? You can't live like this forever."*

- *The person grieving may hear, "You are broken and you are acting in an unacceptable manner."*

> ➤ *"Well, we can't say we didn't expect this, right?"*

- *The person grieving may hear, "Get over it. You knew it was coming, right?" (This may apply in cases of betrayal or loss other than death.)*

What Do We Say
to the Person Grieving?

It is possible to successfully support a grieving person without inflicting further pain.

Here are some examples of support:

➤ *"I don't know what to say. I know you are hurting,"* or *"I can only imagine how you must feel,"* or *"It sounds tough."*

- *The person grieving hears, "You are going through something I don't understand. All I know is you feel hurt and I care and want to help." (Saying these words directly may work best in some circumstances.)*

➤ *"I prayed for you (or your loved one) today."*

- *The person hears, "I care and I trust God to help you through this difficult time."*

➤ *"I am really sorry for your loss."*

- *The person hears, "I care. I am here for you."*

➤ *"It is OK to cry."* *(A phrase generally offered during a comforting hug or after hearing an expression of distress from the grieving person concerning how much they feel like crying during their time of sorrow.)*

- *The person grieving may hear, "You have my permission to express your grief. I am not uncomfortable with it. I understand this is normal and I am glad you are dealing with* it by crying. Cry all you want to and for as long as you need to. I will be here for you." (It may be helpful in some circumstances to say some or all of the things in this paragraph without expecting the grieving person to understand the 'unspoken' messages.)

➤ *"How are you doing?"*

- *The person hears, "I care. I know you are hurting and I am ready to listen to you tell me about your pain if you need support."*

    - *If the grieving person responds briefly with a negative sentence similar to, "Not so good," then to support them we must say another comforting phrase or question them in order to encourage conversation or offer comforting actions and not abandon them at that moment.*

    - *Simply saying "OK. I'm sorry. I will pray," and then walking away will not help much and may make them wonder why you asked how they were doing.*

    - *Any feeling conveyed that your interest is obligatory only may incite resentment instead of comfort.*

    - *A long speech conveying the feeling that the grieving person needs to get over it generally meets resentment though it may not be expressed.*

    - *Comforting actions may include arranging*

to spend time together or reaching out to pray for them at that moment. Though it may take practice to learn to feel comfortable praying with someone, it is well worth the effort.

*   There is nothing so comforting as to feel the power of God flowing over us because of the prayers of a friend during stressful times or when prayer for self is difficult. Sincere, genuine, heartfelt, anointed, prayer filled with compassion is the only kind that makes a difference. Any type of insincerity or perfunctory action is resented.

▪   Comforting words generally include phrases to help the person express their grief even if those phrases are jumbled and don't make much sense.

▪   Words expressing the fact that you care and you are listening may include:

*   "Hmmm . . ."

"What else?"

"Has anything happened recently to make it worse?"

"I hear you and I know you are hurting."

"Oh my. I am so sorry."

"Uh — huh."

"OK."

- *Sometimes it is easier to talk and give advice than it is to listen to the grieving person talk to us. It may sound so negative that we recoil from listening or wonder if it is best for the grieving person to express such negative words. We may even wonder if they are blaming us for their pain.*

- *Validating their feelings as we give them permission to grieve leaves them with the feeling or hope they will recover.*

➤ **There are many more good ideas of what to say to a grieving person, but all of them need to give the person freedom to grieve in their own manner unless the behavior is destructive.**

- *If the grieving person is a lady, they may need to talk more about the problem and simply feel heard and cared for to feel better, even if their words do not make sense at first.*

- *If the person is a man, they may need to do distracting activities or talk about something not connected to help them feel better. In the event that they need advice, talking about the problem helps. Both are helped initially by reminiscing.*

A Sense of Humor

Often having and using our good sense of humor during difficult times makes a big difference. This can be tricky because humor is so varied and many times our sense of humor is not the same as others. Often the use of exaggeration is humorous in a stressful setting. Satire, similes, or comparison used carefully may offer relief from stress. Sarcasm or crude humor rarely is acceptable. Minimizing the pain by using humor often feels like a slap or lack of permission to grieve normally. Slapstick humor may be acceptable if the person is responsive to that type of humor. Here is an example.

A twenty-five year-old daughter, Sandra, lost her brother to AIDS. The day he died and for several days following she felt numb and wandered about like a zombie. Her mother, knowing she often responded to slapstick humor, talked her husband into pretending to surprise her by smashing a pie in her face. The father reluctantly agreed after the mother reassured him there would be no retribution.

That evening he walked into the kitchen when the daughter was present and said to the mother, "I have a surprise for you! Close your eyes." When the mother obeyed he walked up and smashed the pie in her face. The daughter grabbed her face to keep the laughter from exploding and pealing out into the room. She didn't want to make it worse if the mother was upset. As the mother scraped away the whipped cream from her face she said, "Where is Sandra? Is she laughing?"

This idea worked in this case. The slapstick humor released the daughter to give way to her emotions and she began to grieve normally instead of living in the cold, dark world of silence.

Similarity between Laughter and Tears

Laughter and tears are connected because both are a release of intense emotion. Sometimes when we are unable to release the tears normal grieving brings, we may more easily succumb to laughing. Both release stress. Both heavy weeping and audible laughing have similar sounds and use similar bodily functions. Many times it is scarcely discernible when we try to determine if another person is laughing or crying. At times we ask, "Are you crying or laughing?"

Scientists have discovered what Scripture told us long ago—laughter releases toxins from the body. It does as much good as if we had taken a healing tonic.

"A merry heart doeth good like a medicine: but a broken spirit drieth the bones" (Proverbs 17:22).

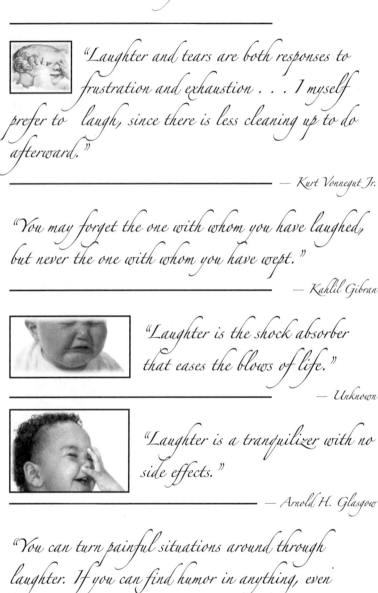

"*Laughter and tears are both responses to frustration and exhaustion . . . I myself prefer to laugh, since there is less cleaning up to do afterward.*"

— *Kurt Vonnegut Jr.*

"*You may forget the one with whom you have laughed, but never the one with whom you have wept.*"

— *Kahlil Gibran*

"*Laughter is the shock absorber that eases the blows of life.*"

— *Unknown*

"*Laughter is a tranquilizer with no side effects.*"

— *Arnold H. Glasgow*

"*You can turn painful situations around through laughter. If you can find humor in anything, even poverty, you can survive it.*"

— *Bill Cosby*

"Laughter is the brush that sweeps away the cobwebs of your heart."

— Mort Walker

"Laughter is the closest distance between two people."

— Victor Borge

"Perhaps I know best why it is man alone who laughs; he alone suffers so deeply that he had to invent laughter."

— Friedrich Nietzsche

"Laughter through tears is my favorite emotion."

— Unknown

"I have seen what a laugh can do. It can transform almost unbearable tears into something bearable, even hopeful."

— Bob Hope

Storms Come to All of Us

If we could, we would shield all of our loved ones from problems or storms. We would eradicate the monster called Grief and send him to a devil's hell. This is not possible. As long as we are in the world we will have tribulation. As long as we suffer we will need support. The sooner and the more effectively we learn to receive support graciously and to offer support to others, the more fulfilled we will feel as we negotiate our friendships and our acquaintances.

> *"These things I have spoken unto you, that in me ye might have peace. In the world ye shall have tribulation: but be of good cheer; I have overcome the world" (John 16:33).*

Points to Ponder

➤ *Often a grieving person is hurt further by those who wish to help the most.*

➤ *Often distance translates emotionally as abandonment or rejection.*

➤ *If we succeed in saying the right words to a friend in need, we have achieved a great feat.*

➤ *Learning to avoid painful phrases is as important as learning to say the right thing.*

➤ *Developing a good sense of humor assists us as we help ourselves and as we reach out to others.*

➤ *Storms of life come to all of us. Our hope is in the Lord.*

Prayers

➤ *Jesus, I have my own personal pain to deal with and I long to help others. Would You help me to refrain from saying things that inflict further pain to others during their time of loss?*

➤ *When I don't know what to say I have a tendency to distance myself from the situation. I know this often translates as rejection or abandonment.*

➤ *Your Word encourages us to learn to say the right thing at the right time. Because of this I know You are there to help us to accomplish it.*

➢ *Lord, help me to study until I understand and learn how to say the right thing at the right time.*

➢ *Jesus, You have given us so many wonderful things to laugh about. I enjoy watching all of the animals you created and how they react to us and to one another. I often smile and think about Your amazing love to us as I hear the birds or smell the flowers.*

➢ *Would You help me to develop a good, creative sense of humor so I will be able to use it to help myself and others during stressful times?*

➢ *Jesus, thank You for making us so wonderfully. I always love to laugh and to cry or to do them at the same time. We are so fearfully and wonderfully made! I love YOU!*

When God Unfolds a Rose

Verse One

There've been times when I thought my prayers
Didn't even reach the ceiling of the room
Where I knelt to pray;
And a voice inside kept asking me
Did I think God was really listening
To anything I had to say.
But I just kept on a praying
And holding on by faith,
Knowing God is always in control.
And I waited like a rosebud in the garden,
For only God can unfold a rose.

Chorus

When God unfolds a rose,
He always gets it right;
When the petals are in place,
Oh, it's such a beautiful sight!
God knows when to hold on
And the perfect time to let go,
So let God have His way
And watch God unfold the rose.

Verse Two

There are trials and tribulations

That we must all go through;

When it comes to heartaches

We've all had our share.

Oh, but when times are the hardest,

We need to hold on to the promise

He said He'd never give us more than we could bear;

So I'll just keep on a praying

And holding on by faith,

Knowing God is working all things for my good

And I'll wait just like a rosebud in the garden,

For only God can unfold a rose.

—*Frank O'Brien*

Nowhere Else to Go by Nathan Greene

"*I pray that our Heavenly Father may assuage the anguish of your bereavement, and leave you only the cherished memory of the loved and lost, and the solemn pride that must be yours to have laid so costly a sacrifice upon the altar of freedom.*"
— *Abraham Lincoln*

pg 109-111 maintaining a grip on Hope
I must walk & pray thru these
difficult days with hope & faith,
GOD knows my problems & has
answered my prayers. P.T.L.
Tom is in the Veterans Home & doing a
well as can be expected. Thank you
Jesus. 12-8-18. Thank you, LORD
for my supporters, Deli Willson,
Stacy Bishop, Sis. Irene Millican,
Sis Bessie Rumph & all the other
Saints, family, Gail & Jay David & his
family, & Leslie, & many more I
don't even know. GOD is good all tim

Pg 117 - Get this book
Pg 120 - Galations 4:4-7 an heir of GOD thru Ch